BLACK YOUTH CRIME

BLACK

THE RUINATION OF A RACE

DAVID ELLSWORTH

DAVID ELLSWORTH

DISCOVERY PRESS
NEW YORK, NY

ISBN -13:9781497394759

DEDICATION

To the dream held by all men of reason,
that opportunity and equality may
come to the land and that
young black men
will have the wisdom
to accept them.

TABLE OF CONTENTS

BLACK

INTRODUCTION

There is a rule of science saying, "Never judge the species by the specimen." And yet we are forced to do just that by the ever increasing number of crimes committed by young black youth.

The growing wave of black violence continues with no one asking why. It continues with no one seeking solutions other than mass arrests. It continues with no indication that the youths themselves understand anything more than the impulse to do harm.

BLACK

Behavior is the mirror in which
everyone shows their image.
Johann Wolfgang von Goethe

THE IMAGE

Orville Lloyd Douglas wrote, "Every time I sit on a crowded street car, bus, or subway train in Toronto, I know I will have an empty seat next to me. It's like a broken record. Sometimes I don't mind having the extra space, but other times I feel awkward, uncomfortable, and annoyed.

"I know I have good hygiene, I dress appropriately, and I mind my own business. However, recently, I finally became cognizant of why people might fear being around me or in close proximity to me: I am a black male. Although Canadian society presents the façade of multiculturalism the truth is Canada has a serious problem with the issue of race.

"I didn't realize it until my sister said to me: Orville, people are afraid of you. You are a six-foot tall black man with broad shoulders.

"My sister is right, people don't sit next to me on the street car, the subway or on the bus because they are afraid. . . ."

Douglas continues with, "I can honestly say I hate being a black male. Although black people like to wax poetic about loving their label I hate 'being black'. I just don't fit into a neat category of the stereotypical views people have of black men. In popular culture black men are recognized in three areas: sports, crime, and entertainment. I hate rap music, I hate most sports, and I like listening to rock music such as PJ Harvey, Morrissey, and Tracy Chapman. I have nothing in common with the archetypes about the black male.

"There is so much negativity and criminal suspicion associated with being a black male in Toronto. Yet, I don't have a criminal record, and I certainly don't associate with criminals. In fact, I abhor violence, and I resent being compared to young black males (or young people of any race) who are lazy, not disciplined, or delinquent. Usually, when black male youth are discussed in Toronto, it is about something going wrong.

"Honestly, who would want to be black? Who would want people to be terrified of you and not want to sit next to you on public transportation? Who would want to have this dark skin, broad nose, large thick lips, and wake up in the morning being despised by the rest of the world?

"A lot of the time I feel like my skin color is like my personal prison, something that I have no control over, for I am judged just because of the way I look.

"Not discussing the issue doesn't mean it is going to go away. In fact, by ignoring the issue, it simply lurks underneath the surface. I believe a dialogue about self-hatred should be brought to the fore in the public sphere, so that some sort of healing and the development of true non-label-based pride can occur.

"Of course, I do not want to have these feelings, to have these dark thoughts about being a black man. However, I cannot deny that this is the way I feel. I don't want to be ashamed of being a black man; I just want to be treated as an individual based on the content of my character, and not just based on the color of my skin."

Undoubtedly, there are millions of black citizens sharing Douglas' opinion. A significant segment of hard working, law abiding Americans are African Americans. and yet, we read in the New York Daily News, "If you're black, you are almost 25 times more likely to be shot in New York City than a white person — and you are also more likely to be arrested for pulling a trigger. Data collected during the first six months of 2013 revealed 74% of the city's 567 shooting victims were black."

Violence by black youth speaks louder than all the acts of good, responsible black citizens. It has created a dynamic and dangerous subculture that breeds violence until it is seen as a natural characteristic of the race. As the violence escalates, the black community has less to say. Only a few responsible representatives like Douglas, have dared express opinions. Another, however, is John McWhorter, black Columbia University professor who after the senseless shooting of Christopher Lane in Oklahoma wrote:

"The numbers don't lie: young black men do commit about 50% of the murders in the U.S. We don't yet know whether the attack on Lane was racially motivated nor can we know whether the three black boys who attacked a white boy on a school bus recently would not have done the same to a black kid. Critics took Al Sharpton and Jesse Jackson to task for not condemning the violence.) But hardly uncommon are cases such as the two black guys who doused a white 13-year-old with gasoline and set him on fire, saying, 'You get what you deserve, white boy' (Kansas City, Mo.) or 20 black kids who beat up Matthew Owens on his porch 'for Trayvon' (Mobile, Ala.)

"So, it's just fake to pretend that the association of young black men with violence comes out of thin air. Young black men murder 14 times more than young white men. If the kinds of things I just mentioned were regularly done by whites, it'd be trumpeted as justification for being scared to death of them.

"It's not that black communities are in complete denial about these statistics — Stop the Violence events are a staple of high-crime areas. But let's face it: black America isn't nearly as indignant about black boys killing one another or whites as about the occasional white cop killing one black boy, even though the former wreaks much more havoc in black communities. There is no coordinated nationwide movement equivalent to the one Martin galvanized. There are no thoughtful films "exploring" black-on-black crime the way Fruitvale Station treats the death of Oscar Grant, a young black man who was killed by transit police in Oakland, Calif.

"And recent example illustrates how many blacks feel about who is murdering whom. Two weeks ago, an NYPD cop killed 14-year-old Shaaliver Douse. Douse was in the process of shooting other people, and had been charged with shooting someone else in May — and yet his aunt compared him to Martin. In her mind, the main sin was the white cop's.

"Granted, it seems a lot easier to do something about the Zimmermans than the black thugs. Protest profiling and police departments institute new programs. But black thugs aren't moved by protests, so it can seem like we're just stuck with them.

"But who's to say what would happen if black America exerted even half of the emotional fervor and brainpower it does over cases like Martin's to thinking about how to keep black boys from going wrong? Annette John-Hall had some wise words on this last year. What kind of self-image do we have to assume we can only change others, but not ourselves?"

McWhorter's appeal for the black community to take action in healing its rising crime rates is countered by a legion of apologists like the NAACP that has dedicated itself to blackwashing the ills of the community at large.

The NAACP has published a litany of crime related facts under the guise that they represent historic wrongs against black people. The fact that African Americans now constitute nearly a million of the 2.3 million persons incarcerated and are put into jails and prisons almost six times the rate of whites is seen as an ugly product of the white man's world.

The JFL Institute publication "Unlocking America" is cited claiming that "if African American and Hispanics were incarcerated at the same rates of whites, today's prison and jail populations would decline by approximately 50%." Strangely, that sounds like another way of saying, "if blacks and Hispanics had lower crime rates, like whites . . . "

Among the laments are that one in six black men has been incarcerated within the past decade and, "If the current trends continue, one in three black males born today can expect to spend time in prison during his lifetime." As if punctuation to the point, the writing adds, "1 in 100 African American women are in prison."

The NAACP points out that, "African Americans serve virtually as much time in prison for a drug offense (58.7 months) as whites do for a violent offense (64,7 months)." This point seems a bit confusing in that it has already been admitted that blacks go to prison at a 6-to-1 rate over whites. That being the case, blacks would obviously have longer rap sheets and prior offenses, thus becoming significant factors to sentencing and time served.

McWhorter mentioned the Christopher Lane killing as a prime example of violence among black youth.

On the afternoon of August 16, 2013, Christopher Lane, 23, left his home to jog around the neighborhood streets. It was his routine and was programmed to keep him in good condition because Lane had dreams waiting to be fulfilled.

He had played baseball in his native Australia for the Essendon Baseball Club and was known as a steady hitter with a good arm. Everyone thought he was good enough to get a college scholarship in the United States and he was willing to give it a try. It didn't take long after arriving in the states for him to obtain a scholarship at East Central University in Ada, Oklahoma. He had shown that he had a all the basic skills and after his first season playing with the ECU Tigers, he was slated to be the starting catcher in the 2014 season. Lane knew that all he had to do was to perform well enough and be diligent about his studies and his dream would be fulfilled. Classmates later told of how he never missed a class and was dedicated to fulfilling his dream of returning to Australia with a U.S. degree and playing baseball again in his homeland. It was apparent that he would probably marry his girlfriend, Sarah Harper. Things were very serious between the two, especially after taking a trip to Australia together.

But on that August day he closed the door behind him and started to find his jogging rhythm along the sidewalks of the peaceful streets of Duncan, Oklahoma.

There was a lot to like about Duncan. Its residential areas feature myrtle trees and a lush green landscape. Not being an American, Lane couldn't appreciate that Duncan was born as a layover on the old Chisholm Trail or that it was the home of Erle P. Halliburton, founder of the Halliburton Oil Well Cementing Company that was later to raise scandalous questions about Iraq and Richard Cheney. For Lane, however, it was where Sarah, his American girlfriend lived. They had returned from Australia the week before and he was in Duncan visiting her parents. In a couple of weeks he would have returned to his university in Ada, some 85 miles away.

On this August day, however, he had found his pace and moved briskly along Country Club Road. He didn't notice when a black Ford Focus came up behind him. He only felt a sharp impact in his back and suddenly his body wouldn't respond as it should. He screamed with pain and anguish and fell to his knees. Moments later he struggled to his feet, took a couple of steps before collapsing into a shallow ditch next to the sidewalk. A .22 caliber bullet had penetrated both of his lungs and punctured his pulmonary artery.

Joyce Smith was driving in the area that afternoon and saw Lane lying in the ditch with blood on the back of his shirt. She immediately called 911 and gave them the basic details. Others appeared on the scene, two of them construction workers who heard a shot and saw a black car driving away. Another woman who had stopped to investigate was giving Lane CPR. All were waiting for the sound of sirens and Smith, still connected to the 911 operator, said frantically, "If they don't come soon, he's gone."

Within minutes Detective John Byers arrived at the scene. The 911 dispatcher had said the victim had been shot and he knew the importance of preserving a crime scene. Investigators went to nearby Don Jose's Mexican Restaurant on Highway 81 and asked to review the security camera tapes. Within minutes they were watching a black hatchback auto pass the crime scene before entering the restaurant parking lot and then moving to the parking area of the Duncan Inn Hotel where it remained for 11 minutes before driving away out of camera view.

A copy of the security video was taken to the police department where Detective Holly Atkinson recognized the car as being very similar to one driven by Michael Jones. Atkinson had encountered Jones in a prior investigation and pulled out the report to note the license number of the vehicle, 296FLG.

Five hours after the shooting, the department received another call, this time from James Johnson complaining that there were young men at his residence with firearms, the official affidavit reports:

"At approximately 1905 hours on August 16, 2013, Master Officer Ryan Atkinson was dispatched to a call at 111 West Ash where James Johnson had advised that there were juveniles with guns at his residence. When M.O. Atkinson arrived at the scene he observes Jones and three other males outside of Jones car in the Immanuel Baptist Church parking lot located at 2nd Street and Ash, Duncan, Stephens County, Oklahoma. M.O. Atkinson knew Jones from a prior contact and also knew James Edwards. M.O. Atkinson then made contact with them and all parties were not being cooperative and then M.O. Atkinson contacted your affiant (Detective John Byers) and asked if we were looking for a small black car in the shooting I was currently investigating. I advised him that I was still working the crime scene and he called Detectives and the Police Department. Later all four persons were transported to the Duncan Police Department for interviews, and the car was secured pending a search warrant."

Those taken into custody were Chancey Luna, 16 and James Edwards, 15, both black students at a local high school. With them was Michael Jones, 17, white. The initial interrogations came up with very little information with Jones wanting a lawyer and Luna claiming he wasn't in the car at the time of the shooting and Jones had merely given him a ride to the courthouse. Jones, however, was more cooperative, admitting that he was driving when someone fired a shot. He was not willing to say who it was because he "didn't want to be killed." Later he would reveal that they parked behind the hotel so Chancey Luna could remove the cold air induction and hide the gun inside.

When the search warrant was gained, the gun was found where Jones had stated and police knew they had found their source of information that would convict Luna and Edwards. In the trunk of the car police found a dismantled shotgun and linked it to a dead donkey that had been slain with a shotgun only a block away from the Lane crime scene. Investigators also learned that the trio had been waiting in the church parking lot for the arrival of Christopher Johnson, a local youth who had been slated as their next victim. By all appearances, a killing spree had been avoided by valid information from witnesses and quick action by the investigators.

Duncan is a typical community of less than 25,000 residents of which only 3.3% are black. In spite of their low contribution to the population, three teenagers, two of them black, decided to kill someone on that bright August day.

Three days earlier, 15-year-old James Edwards Jr., tweeted, "With my niggas when it's time to start taken life's," and news reports said it was a line from a Chief Keef rap song, "I Don't Like." Three and a half months earlier Edwards had tweeted that he hated white people. Videos of Edwards and Chancey Luna showed both with large amounts of cash, leading authorities to speculate their possible involvement in drug dealing. Edwards and Chancey Luna, 16, would be charged as adults with first degree murder. The following day their mug shots would appear in an Australian newspaper under the heading, *The Faces of Evil* and the Prime Minister of Australia would be warning citizens to consider twice before visiting the United States.

The investigation probed into the social media used by the suspects. Facebook photos showed the two black suspects displaying gang signs with hand signals, holding large bundles of cash to their ears as if it was a telephone and playing the gangsta roles with guns in videos. Edwards had changed his profile photo only seven days earlier to show his face hidden behind a blue scarf, the same as would a member of the Crips gang. Local rumors had it that both Edwards and Luna were trying to join the Crips and authorities confirm that the Crips are active in Oklahoma.

It was also revealed that the trio had been fans of violent video games and enchanted with rap music, especially that of Chief Keef, a reportedly illiterate rapster whose website features his tattoos, profanity, photos of him with an AK47 and generally a promotion of the gangsta lifestyle. Some of his lyrics have phrases like "shoot on sight," which is what Chancey Luna did. One of the startling interrogation responses was "We were bored and decided to kill someone."

Chief Keef, whose real name is Keith Cozart, includes details like, ". . . he was a legend among kids on the South Side of Chicago, a gritty set of neighborhoods that most recently made the news for its astonishing rise in murder rate (up 38% in 2012 alone). On December 4, 2011, at age 16, Keef was shot at by police and arrested for unlawful use of a weapon and subsequently placed under house arrest, at his grandmother's house, for a month."

Any rational person would ask, if he had never made a rap recording at the time, how was he a "legend among kids on the South Side?" The implication is clear. A 15-year-old dropout having a shootout with police presents the gangsta image he raps about to the detriment of youngsters like Edwards and Luna. He was a legend as a thug.

Only months before the famous Trayvon Martin case of a black young man being slain by a white neighborhood watch leader, had brought international marches and protests. President Obama had decided to join in with his comment, "You know, when Trayvon Martin was first shot I said that this could have been my son" But now no one was speaking. White House reporters asked why the president was silent about the Christopher Lane case and received a cursory reply. White House spokesman Josh Earnest said he wasn't familiar with the case. Al Sharpton, American Baptist minister, civil rights activist, said following the jury's verdict finding Zimmerman innocent, "I think that this is an atrocity, it is probably one of the worst situations that I have seen. What this jury has done is establish a precedent that when you are young and fit a certain profile, you can be committing no crime ... and be killed and someone can claim self-defense ... we had to march to even get a trial and even at trial, when he's exposed over and over again as a liar, he is acquitted."

The Trayvon Martin case had been blown into an international fervor and now there was silence. The president had nothing to say. Sharpton issued no statement. Jesse Jackson had tweeted, "Praying for the family of Chris Lane. This senseless violence is frowned upon and the justice system must prevail."

Frowned upon? The comment seemed a bit diluted for the severity of the crime. Instead of addressing the problem of mounting black violence across the nation, Jackson chose to point to two white men in Oklahoma who the year before had killed three blacks in an apparent hate motivated rampage.

Fox News' Michelle Malkin accused black leaders of speaking out only when it was personally convenient and called Jackson's 'frowned upon' comment "underwhelming."

"They always have something to say about the most trivial things if it serves their political agenda," Malkin stated. "This is an atrocity that everyone should be condemning from the top of their lungs. This guy (Jackson) can't even get it up with his finger to wag it with any sort of conviction.

"It shows you that these race hustlers have absolutely no commitment to principle and cannot transcend their own racial narrow agenda."

If black leaders wanted Malkin to be wrong, they weren't doing much to prove it. Not long before, when speaking of the Trayvon Martin case, Jackson had been fiercely vocal saying, "Blacks are under attack!" he added, "Our disparities are great," he said. "Targeting, arresting, convicting blacks and ultimately killing us is big business."

The black community wanted the world to see Trayvon as an innocent kid walking home from a store while much of the white community saw a black mother kicking her son out of the house to live with his father who was busy with his lover at the time. They saw a kid suspended from school, suspected by police, posing with gang signals, implanting gold onto his teeth to have the gang image and telling his girlfriend about a cracker following him. Jackson's message that "Blacks are under attack" somehow didn't ring any truer than his claim from years before that Martin Luther King had died in his arms.

Only four weeks before the senseless slaying of Christopher Lane, three black teenagers attacked a white 13-year-old on a school bus in Florida. The assault was triggered because the white youngster had told school authorities that one of the black youths had tried to sell him drugs. He was beaten and kicked mercilessly to the point that the adult bus driver was "petrified" and afraid to intervene.

At the court hearing on the matter, one of the fathers of the black attackers claimed his son was sorry for the attack. "This is life," he said, "I am sorry what happened to the victim. It's just the way it is."

The way it is? Where is a three-on-one beating by bigger, older assailants dismissed as "the way it is?" The allegation of selling drugs is so easily treated as being part of the cultural norm? The three assailants, identified as Joshua Reddin, Julian McKnight and Lloyd Khemradj, all 15 – two years older than their victim – had planned and executed a criminal act. Reddin was also charged with unarmed robbery since he took the victim's cell phone and money after the attack.

Ex-Florida Rep. Allen West was also critical of Al Sharpton and Jesse Jackson because they had been extremely vocal about the Trayvon Martin case but now had nothing to say. He wrote in his Facebook page, "Three 15-yr-old black teens beat up a 13-yr-old white kid because he told school officials they tried to sell him drugs. Do you hear anything from Sharpton, Jackson, NAACP, Stevie Wonder, Jay-Z, liberal media, or Hollywood? Cat got your tongues or is it that pathetic hypocrisy revealing itself once again? Y'all just make me sick."

In typical style, Jesse Jackson responded by telling of his alleged atrocities toward blacks instead of addressing the immediate problem involving a white victim. He had done the same thing when dealing with the Christopher Lane case.

"Last year, 135 blacks were killed, black men, unarmed, killed by vigilantes, police, killed by security guards, so whether it's the case of Oakland, Calif., or the case in New York, it's just too much of it. Wherever it occurs, it must always be discouraged; there must be a deterrent from it occurring. We must urge people to live in civilized ways."

One must question how the 135 blacks allegedly killed by vigilantes, police and security guards equates with the 680 murder victims of black crime in the cities of Chicago and Detroit alone? Jackson repeats with boring consistency, however, that these cases cannot be compared to Trayvon Martin. He made the claim with Christopher Lane's murder and again about the school bus beating. So what does equate with the Trayvon case? After all, the court decided that Martin had, in fact, been the aggressor and should we ignore that he posed for photos to be posted in Facebook with a wad of money and another with arms just as had Edwards and Luna, all in the style of the gangsta rage among young blacks?

Jackson and Sharpton were also silent in 2007 when four black men and one black woman participated in the savage torture and slaying of Channon Gail Christian and Hugh Christopher Newsom, Jr.

The case, for all its viciousness and horror, gained little attention from the national media.   Unlike the Trayvon case, none of the national organizations protested or demanded action.   The president of Criminal Justice Journalists said, "I can't say that this one would have had any more coverage if five whites had been accused of doing these things to two blacks, absent a blatant racial motive... as bad as this crime is, the apparent absence of any interest group involvement or any other 'angle' might also explain the lack of coverage."

In keeping with the Jackson philosophy of promoting the black agenda in the face of atrocities involving white victims, Leonard Pitts, Pulitzer Prize winning black syndicated columnist wrote:

"It always amazes me when white people put on the victim hat. As in victim of racial oppression. By any measure – health, education, economics, employment – white Americans enjoy a superior standard of living. If that's racial oppression, sign me up.

"But still, one occasionally hears mewling noises from that subset of my white countrymen who feel put-upon by big, bad racial minorities.

"And Knoxville, Tenn., has become the capital city of that lunatic fringe.

"It seems that in January, a young white couple, Channon Christian and Christopher Newsom, were victims of a brutal crime. They were carjacked, kidnapped and raped. Cleaning fluid was sprayed into Christian's mouth. She was stuffed in a trash can and apparently suffocated. Newsom was shot and set afire. His body was dumped. Five blacks, one a woman, have been arrested. [Now compare this to the fake Duke Lacrosse Rape and the media coverage it enjoyed].

19

"The story made headlines around Knoxville. It was unnoticed nationally.

"That has changed. A constellation of white supremacists and conservative bloggers has pushed the story into the national limelight as illustration of their argument that news media, constrained by political correctness, refuse to report black-on-white crime while pulling out all the stops when crime is white on black, as in the Duke University lacrosse debacle. I would see their Duke case and raise them a Central Park jogger, but what do I know?

Anyway, bloggers such as Michael Oliver have chastised the "liberal, biased, mainstream media" for missing the Knoxville story. He asked, "Had the roles been reversed, would the media ignore such a horrific crime?"

"Truth is, media ignore horrific crimes all the time. Space is limited and growing more so. Which means the story that catches fire usually has some element beyond gruesomeness to sell it. In the Duke case, it was class, privilege, sex and race that did it.

"Not that I expect Oliver or other "oppressed" white people to pay attention to something so trivial as fact. They're too busy demanding that this case be tried as a hate crime – even though police say there's no evidence the couple were targeted for any other reason than that they were there. And on May 26, white supremacists held – I kid you not – a "rally against genocide" in Knoxville.

"Part of me thinks I should consider the source and let this slide. But the argument being advanced here is so utterly, abysmally, stupidly, self-servingly wrong that I cannot help but respond.

"Black crime against whites is underreported? On what planet? Study after study and expert after expert tell a completely different story.

"For instance, there's 'Off Balance: Youth, Race and Crime in the News,' a 2001 report that concluded: Blacks and Latinos are underrepresented in news media as victims of crime and significantly overrepresented as perpetrators, based on crime statistics; newspaper articles about white homicide victims are longer and more frequent than those about black ones; and interracial violent crime is more likely to be reported, even though it is just about the rarest kind of violent crime.

"And here I'm obligated, because I'm black, to say that if the defendants in this case did what they are accused of doing, I'd be happy to see them rot under the jailhouse. Sadly, that needs saying, because there are people who will not take it as a given.

"But with that obligation fulfilled, let me add that I am likewise unkindly disposed toward the crackpots, incendiaries and flat-out racists who have chosen this tragedy upon which to take an obscene and ludicrous stand.

"I have four words for them and any other white Americans who feel themselves similarly victimized: Cry me a river."

To many readers, Pitts' cold and uncompassionate treatment of the case only unified his mentality with that of the perpetrators. His use of 'Off Balance: Youth, Race and Crime in the News' as an authoritative reference ignored the subsequent study, 'Sentence Severity and Crime: Accepting the Null Hypothesis' by Anthony N. Doob and Cheryl M. Webster that effectively criticized its methodology and findings. To suggest that the case would have been ignored had it not been for "A constellation of white supremacists and conservative bloggers" is easily translated as being undeserving of public attention. In reality, the nation had seen few murders so brutal and killers so animalistic.

Yes, some bloggers were asking why the case had not drawn more attention, especially after the international exposure given to the Trayvon Martin case. Wasn't the Martin case in the news for the exact reason Pitts complained about? It was driven into public attention by black organizations and black leaders using the tragedy for the very reasons Malkin mentioned, self-serving interests.

Without receiving attention from the media, bloggers decided to put the details of the crime before the public eye.

It wasn't pretty.

On the night of Saturday, January 6, 2007, Christopher Newsom and his girlfriend Channon Christian went out together for the last time. Newsom was a 23-year-old carpenter; Christian a 21-year-old senior majoring in sociology at the University of Tennessee. The couple had been dating for about two months and seemed very much smitten with each other. That Saturday night, the couple had eaten a romantic dinner at a Knoxville restaurant. Channon last spoke with her mother Denna at roughly 12:35 a.m. on Sunday when Channon said the couple was going to visit a friend to watch some movies. They were never heard from again.

At 12:24 pm Sunday, Christopher's burned corpse was found by a Norfolk Southern railroad employee near the railroad tracks in a rough area on the north side of Knoxville, Tennessee. The next day Channon's Toyota 4-Runner was located a few blocks away — it was actually found by Channon's parents who were canvassing the area after the cell phone company gave police the last known location of their daughter's cell phone. Channon was nowhere to be found, but crime scene technicians lifted a print from an envelope found in the SUV. Analysis matched the print to Lemaricus Davidson, a recently-released ex-con living in the area. Knoxville police and Knox County Sheriff's Department investigators got a search warrant for Davidson's home at 2316 Chipman Street — by Tuesday at 2 pm, they located Channon Christian's body in a kitchen trash bin. The house was a rental property but the renters were gone.

Police were left with two corpses of a young couple who had been tortured and killed in the most brutal fashion anyone in Knoxville could remember.

As information slowly emerged out of the investigation, it was clear this was on ordinary crime. "It apparently started with a carjacking," said U.S. Marshal Rich Knighten, "They did some really nasty things to this lady. There is some evidence she was held and sexually abused for a couple of days." In fact, as police gathered more facts it became clear that both Newsom and Christian were brutalized beyond imagination.

In the wee hours of that Sunday morning, Newsom and Christian were carjacked at gunpoint in her parents' 2005 Toyota 4-Runner and brought back to the house on Chipman. Christopher Newsom was raped over and over again (semen was found in his anus) and sodomized with an unknown object. He was blindfolded, gagged, and bound at the hands and feet. After several nightmarish hours, Newsom was either walked barefoot or dragged out to the railroad tracks where he was shot in the back of the head execution-style. The assailants shot him two more times (in the back and in the neck). Then Newsom's corpse was doused with gasoline and lit on fire.

For Channon Christian, the torture was even worse. She suffered days of sexual abuse in the Chipman home. She was beaten mercilessly and raped numerous times, suffering excruciating injuries to her mouth, vagina, and anus. Forensic pathologists found that not only was Christian raped by her captors, but she had been penetrated with an object as well (possibly a chair leg, according to the Knox County Medical Examiner). In addition, examiners found that a chemical (likely bleach) had been poured down her throat and in her wounded genital areas — while she was still alive. The coroner reported that Christian was then tied up with torn strips of bedding, her head covered in a white garbage bag — and then the whole body stuffed in five larger trash bags before being thrown into a garbage can. Perhaps the most horrifying finding was that Christian was still alive at the time; her death came after the slow process of suffocation in that trash container.

Police immediately began searching for the renter of 2316 Chipman Street, a convicted felon named Lemaricus Davidson. Davidson had recently finished a five-year prison sentence for a previous carjacking and robbery charge. Law enforcement also sought Davidson's brother Letalvis Cobbins. By Wednesday, January 11, 2007, authorities had arrested Davidson in Knoxville; Cobbins and his friend George Thomas were picked up by US Marshals in Lebanon, Kentucky. Further investigation led to the arrest of Cobbins' girlfriend Vanessa Coleman, who witnessed the kidnapped couple in the house on Chipman Street. On January 31, 2007, a grand jury handed down a 46-count indictment against the four defendants.

The attackers would be tried separately, but the first person convicted in the case would be a man who had no contact with Newsom or Christian. Dewayne Boyd was convicted by a Federal jury on April 16, 2008 as an accessory to the carjacking for his role in hiding Davidson in the days after the killings. He would be sentenced to 18 years in prison.

On August 25, 2009, a Davidson County jury (there was too much media coverage to find an impartial jury in Knox County, so a jury was bused in from Nashville where there had been less publicity, and sequestered) convicted 26-year-old Letalvis Cobbins of the first-degree murder and rape of Channon Christian (he was acquitted of the Newsom rape counts and convicted of a lesser facilitation charge in regard to Newsom's death). Prosecutors had called Cobbins the second-in-command during the crimes, and had used forensic investigation to link Cobbins' DNA to the victims' remains. Cobbins took the stand in his own defense, telling jurors that he had consensual oral sex with Christian — offered with the promise that he would set her free afterward. But he conceded that he left her in captivity afterward — and admitted that he was present when Christian was stuffed in the garbage can and left to die. Jurors ultimately opted to spare Cobbins from the death penalty and instead found he should be sentenced to life imprisonment without the possibility of parole.

The next defendant to stand trial was 28-year-old Lemaricus Davidson, the man who rented the house in which the crimes took place and who, prosecutors said, planned the rapes and murders. At trial, the State linked Davidson to a fingerprint in Christian's Toyota and to the gun believed to be the murder weapon in Newsom's murder. Davidson's DNA was found on Christian, but not on Newsom. On October 28, 2009, Davidson was convicted on 35 of 38 total counts — he was not convicted of raping Newsom — including the first-degree murders of both victims. The penalty phase started the next day; the jury was sent back to decide Davidson's fate on October 30, 2009. After approximately three hours of deliberation, the panel sentenced the ringleader to death by lethal injection.

George Thomas, 26, was a friend of Letalvis Cobbins and the third man to be tried for the murder/rape of Christian and Newsom. Thomas' defense attorneys had the best shot at an acquittal thus far as there was no DNA, fingerprint or eyewitness evidence against their client. Thomas had admitted being in the Chipman Street house at the time, but denied taking part in any crimes against the couple. Regardless, the evidence was strong enough for a Hamilton County jury to hand down 38 guilty verdicts, including first-degree murder, rape, robbery, and kidnapping. The verdict came on December 8, 2009 — two days later that same jury recommended Thomas serve a sentence of life imprisonment with no chance of parole.

The last trial would be the most difficult for prosecutors. 21-year-old Vanessa Coleman, Letalvis Cobbins' girlfriend, admitted being at the house and witnessing the strangling of Channon Christian. But she said she was paralyzed by fear, that she had been threatened with harm if she tried to leave and alert authorities. Moreover, there was no forensic evidence linking her to either victim. On May 13, 2010, Coleman was acquitted of the first-degree murder of Christian and of all charges pertaining to Newsom. However, she was convicted of facilitation in the murder and rapes of Christian. On July 30, 2010, Judge Richard Baumgartner rejected the defense's plea for leniency and sentenced Coleman to 53 years behind bars.

With the last of the trials done and the defendants behind bars for decades, the terrible story seemed to be over. But this case had been sensational from the start... and there would be more controversy to come.

Although the horrors inflicted upon Channon Christian and Christopher Newsom were luridly savage, the national news media was slow to pick up the story. Conservative commentators and right-wing blogs insisted that the crimes were being ignored by mainstream media out of a perverse sense of political correctness — simply because the victims were white and the suspects were black. TV pundit and conservative columnist Michelle Malkin said "There is a discomfort level with stories that have black assailants and white victims... If it doesn't fit some sort of predetermined narrative of how we view taboo subjects like race and crime, there's a disinclination to cover it."

The controversy over the media's treatment of the killings spilled onto the streets of Knoxville on May 26, 2007, when 30 or so white supremacists gathered to protest the perceived lack of coverage. Hal Turner, an internet talk show host, summed up the protest's objectives with abrasive rhetoric: "The goal of this rally is twofold: We want to tell the liberal media we are tired of them spiking stories about black-on-white crime. Our second goal is to tell the black community they have to restrain their black hoodlums." The public statement was far different from what Pitts called a "rally against genocide" that he found "abysmally, stupidly, self-servingly wrong."

A throng of social activists calling themselves the Coup Cluts Clowns showed up in clown make-up to stage a counter-protest. Although Knoxville police deemed the event "fairly orderly", they ended up arresting white supremacist organizer Alex Linder for disorderly conduct and resisting arrest.

For its part, prosecutors denied the crimes, while undeniably appalling in nature, should be considered hate crimes. "We have no evidence to support the notion that this was a race-based crime," said Knoxville police chief Sterling Owen, "we see this as a cold-blooded murder." Those beliefs were echoed by Knox County DA Randy Nichols: "It was a terrible crime, a horrendous crime, but race was not a motive. We know from our investigation that the people charged in this case were friends with white people, socialized with white people, dated white people... there is no evidence of any racial animus, there's evidence to the contrary."

The families of the victims seemed somewhat conflicted about the issue of hate crime. Channon's father Gary Christian told reporters: "There are people out there that just want to make something even worse than what it already is... I think any kind of crime like that's a hate crime. Was it racial? No I don't think so." Christopher's parents were less certain. Hugh Newsom opined to a local TV reporter, "Would they have done that to a black couple? I don't think so." Christopher's mother Mary added: "With all the things they did to them, what else could you call it but hate?"

Knox County Criminal Court Judge Richard Baumgartner presided over all four high-profile trials of the Christian-Newsom murder defendants. Promoted to the bench in 1992, Baumgartner had served without incident through most of the next two decades. But court watchers noted the judge could seem dazed and impaired at times. In 2010, Judge Baumgartner caused awkward moments just before the announcement of the jury's decision in the trial of Vanessa Coleman — as he stumbled to correctly read over the verdict form. In January 2011, Baumgartner made a surprise decision to take a medical leave. That news was quickly followed by revelations that the judge was under criminal investigation. The Tennessee Bureau of Investigation (TBI) had found evidence that Baumgartner had obtained prescription pain medication from a felon named Christopher Lee Gibson — whose probation came before Judge Baumgartner. By March 2011, Judge Baumgartner had pled guilty to felony official misconduct. All of his prior cases would be put under strict scrutiny from defense attorneys and prosecutors alike.

On December 1, 2011, Special Judge Jon Kerry Blackwood ruled that the trials of all four defendants, Lemaricus Davidson, Letalvis Cobbins, George Thomas, and Vanessa Coleman, had been "structurally flawed" by Baumgartner's on-bench intoxication and would have to be done all over again. Citing the TBI probe into Baumgartner's pill-popping, Judge Blackwood said: "He committed a crime every day. That's every day he's sitting on this bench in this robe. There is no other conclusion this court can make but that there was structural error." That the cases would have to be tried again was bad news for prosecutors, but there was a more immediate effect as well: because 3 of the 4 juries had rejected the death penalty already, only Davidson could face the ultimate punishment in his retrial.

The decision to hold retrials for Cobbins, Davidson, and Thomas (the decision to retry Coleman was not appealed) was affirmed in a split decision by the Tennessee Court of Criminal Appeals on April 13. In May of 2012, the Tennessee Supreme Court overturned Blackwood's ruling ordering new trials for Cobbins, Davidson, and Thomas, commenting that its "order should not be construed as condoning or excusing" Baumgartner's misconduct.

In June 2012, prosecutors filed to have Judge Blackwood recused from the case after he invoked the "13th juror rule" " to reverse himself and decline to grant new trials for Cobbins and Davidson (the motion for recusal also applies to Thomas' case, although he was still set to have a retrial). The motion cited Blackwood's emotional involvement in the case as potentially interfering with a fair trial. Following Blackwood's recusal, Senior Judge Walter Kurtz was named to oversee the retrials and the decisions to grant them. Ultimately, retrials were denied for Cobbins and Davidson, but a retrial was granted for Thomas. (Coleman's retrial was unaffected by the motions.)

Facing the same charges from the first trial, on November 20, 2012, Vanessa Coleman was convicted by a mixed-race jury of facilitation of aggravated kidnapping, facilitation of rape, and the facilitation of the murder of Channon Christian, but not of Christopher Newsom. These convictions were on lesser charges than her initial convictions. While the retrial remained in Knoxville, the jury for the retrial was selected from Jackson in western Tennessee, over 300 miles west of Knoxville on I-40. Judge Blackwood sentenced Coleman to 35 years in prison on February 1, 2013, minus credit for time already served. Coleman will be eligible for parole in early 2019.

On May 17, 2013, the retrial of George Thomas (with a jury empaneled in Nashville ended in a verdict of guilty on all counts with a lesser charge on count 17. He was re-sentenced to life in prison by the jury, but this time with the possibility of parole after 51 years. On June 4, 2013, George Thomas was given two life sentences (consecutive) for the murders and 25 years (multiple concurrent) for the rapes by Senior Judge Walter Kurtz.

Lemaricus Davidson pled guilty to a robbery that took place in a Knoxville Pizza Hut on January 8, 2007 — just a day after the killings. He received a sentence of eight years for the robbery — that time will not be added to whatever punishment he is meted in his murder/rape retrial. The sentences will run concurrently.

While the families of Channon Christian and Christopher Newsom relived the tragic events again and again in a series of retrials, supporters were able to remember the loss in a positive way. On March 26, 2012, the Chris Newsom Memorial Baseball Tournament was held at Halls Community Park in Knoxville. Proceeds from gate fees and t-shirt sales were put into a scholarship fund in Newsom's name to provide scholarships for graduating seniors of Halls High School, Newsom's alma mater.

The story had been covered by both local and national media but not with the intensity of something like the Duke University rape case, in which three white students were charged with raping a black stripper at a party in March, 2006. All the charges against the students were eventually dropped but the case generated a lot of visibility and controversy along racial lines. This case had featured a white on black crime and was highly publicized even though Leonard Pitts insisted it was because of, "class, privilege, sex and race . . ."

The fact remains that the murders of Newsom and Christian have become better known through forwarded e-mails and blogs than from national media. It would be difficult, however, to argue that it is because of racial bias. The O.J. Simpson murder trial was one of the most intensively covered crimes involving a black defendant with white victims.

Rich Buhler, the founder of TruthOrFiction.com, has worked in the news media for more than 40 years and said, "There are heartbreaking and horrifying crimes all over the nation every day that you don't hear about until, for example, you watch a true crime show or read a true crime book. Newsom and Christian were not only victims of human monsters but also became crime statistics that are, very tragically, all too common."

Let us assume that Buhler and Pitts are correct and many horrifying crimes go unmentioned in national media. That would only amplify the social impact of black crime in America. If black men are given the image of dangerous predators in the nation's streets because of crime stories appearing in the media, then they should be feared even more when considering all the unreported crimes and those not being publicized.

The failure to address problems confronting the black community has caused the race to be identified by its minority and characterized by violence and crime. The race in general was identified by one poster responding to the question of "why I hate blacks" with:

"I don't hate black people either. I just get sick and tired of the NAACP, Black TV, King Day, The racism call all the time, Black History Month, Black Panthers, Black USA Pageant, You Owe Me and many more.

"I guess I could sum it up with one word, "crime, crime, crime, crime." Violent black behavior. In other words, 'you people,' have ruined this country, and we 'white people' are sick of it. Black over breeding of their own species annoys us. These stupid mult-syllable invented names that 'you people' now go by. Not speaking or talking in a manner consistent with intelligent human verbal communication. I want to "axe" you a question, really kills me. It is "ask" rather than "axe." Riding around town with that gangsta hip-hop ghetto thug music blaring out of a tacky vehicle. I could do this all day. By the way, I am caucasion, and I voted for Barack Obama in 2008."

Some responses were more personal in nature. "I am married to a black man and it is all the reasons stated above if you want equality why is there a black history month but no white history month? Why is a business made to keep a certain number of minority employees but not white employees? Why do blacks get more grant money for going to a predominately white school? Why does every black person think that everything they go through (is) the white man's fault? Blacks are given every opportunity a white person is given they would rather take advantage of the system like food stamps, Tenncare, etc. rather than take advantage of an education that the state would pay for them to get. All my schooling was paid for by grants and I don't have any kids. Most of them are lazy and expect the white man to pay taxes and take care of them while they collect food stamps, insurance, and section 8. Laziness and crime are the main reason the black population is slowly killing itself off with all the black on black crime. The two black men killed at the Wolfe Building were killed by two other black men? Do you get it now?"

The black race, regardless of its historic character, is quickly becoming identified by a growing, defiant, gang cultured segment of its youth. And instead of developing plans and programs to address the problem, black leaders remain dedicated to being apologists or fabricating an image of whites as the enemy.

The willingness to ignore fact and create false scenarios, motives and participation never reached more disgusting heights than in the case of Channon Christian and Chris Newsom. Years after the crime, the website "blackmalefelon" was incredibly placing the blame on the victim.

"Would black on white (BOW) crime poster child Channon Christian be proud that one of her alleged rapists and killers is reportedly still, six years later, considered one of America's sexiest BOW rapists by her own, racially terroristic and psychotically deranged white Americans?

"Christian, who a GhettoBraggingRights (GBR) street investigation determined purchased (and) arranged her and a male friend's carjacking, kidnapping, robbery and rape under the delusion of getting the whole black thug sexual experience, is believed to have killed her male companion and committed suicide in a black sex driven, drug fueled escape.

"White America (males, females, boys and girls) went crazy over Letalvis," new GBR publisher Aniga Shakur says. "There were white kids and young adults allegedly dressing like Channon and her friend on Halloween and going to the house where they believed consensual gang bang happened and there's even the alleged Channon Christian Black Male Thug Sex Death Cult that young white males and females around the country are reportedly joining in masses."

One can only imagine what degree of ignorance and disregard for the feelings of the victims' families would create such wholesale fabrications and malicious lies. In response to inexcusable acts of violence, black publications only recommend more violence.

Black killer Adrian Barker stomped white Christopher Kernich unconscious in front of 17 witnesses in Kent, Ohio in 2009. Kernich died six days later and Barker was subsequently found guilty. While doctors were frantically trying to save Kernich's life, the radical black site underprivilegedmedianetwork.com declared, "It's war. With potentially thousands of whites and so called brainwashed blacks said to be hoping and praying for popular Kent State University student Chris Kernich to have a full recovery from injuries he received after allegedly thinking "nigger," hundreds of Akron, Cleveland and, reportedly, an emerging brotherhood of Kent State Black Foot Soldiers joined to protest *any* recovery and to condemn whites who think it's *okay* to *think* nigger."

According to the hate filled website, Kernich "thought" the word nigger and thus deserved to die. It is not explained how anyone would know what Kernich was thinking but apparently those in charge of the website believe it's possible since they claimed, "The elders, however, are now asking for brother and sisters who heard Kernich think the "nigger" word or other vile thoughts to come forward." It is not clear who the elders are but it is claimed that an "army of black foot soldiers" exists and are led by elders such as Elohim Belial who heads the God Damn White America Movement.

Those writing the underprivilegedmedianetwork.com content contaminate young black minds into believing that by subscribing to such hate, they join into an organization where violence, spiritualism and holy justification are gained. To believe that someone is empowered to kill because they can perceive thoughts reaches into a depth of ignorance that finds no excuse.

It was Anika Shakur who used her website to proclaim, "We know now that when any atrocity befalls any white person at the hands of any person of color it is in accordance with the edict and bounty the universe has issued against them for their Universal Law violations, failure to make restitution for their racial crimes and crimes against the planet."

Reasonable writings recognize that rebellious black youth do not represent their race as a whole while black publications produce writings such as the above under the title, "No Whites Are Innocent." Blacks at large ask that they not be judged by the violence committed by a minority yet modern whites are judged by the acts of whites in the 18th century.

In 2010, Michael Jerome Lee, 20, and his friends, Bo Ellis Taylor, 19, Jamal Breon Lang, 21, and Ernest Teryl Wiggins, 20 were driving around hunting for someone to rob when they followed someone leaving an ATM machine. The person was Christopher Kyser Miree's roommate who entered the home and left soon after. Miree, white, was a graduate student at Vanderbilt University and had a job. He was alone when the four knocked on the door and burst into the house, stole one hundred dollars from Miree before Lee shot him in the head as he begged for his life.

Black radicals dealt with the case in websites stating, "Alabama Black Foot Soldiers have reportedly condemned the arrest of four Reparations Protesters being held for the April 16 alleged robbery and slaying of 23 year old Kyser Miree, a *privileged* Vanderbilt Magna Cum Laude graduate whose family is believed to have owned slaves during the Trans Atlantic Slave Trade. Black Foot Soldier publisher Yusef Douglas reports:

"(T)he Slaves Schedules of the 1850 census, Wm. S. Miree of Perry County Alabama (Only 1 county removed from Jeffereson County Alabama – which Birmingham resides) owned a considerable number of slaves.

"Reparations protesters Jamal Breon Lang, 20; Michael Jerome Lee, 19; Bo Taylor, 18; and Earnest Teryl Wiggins, 19 are currently being held for the protest which, according to Mobile Black Foot Soldier Moses Abernathy, Reparations Offender Miree is believed to have turned violent."

The support of mindless violence with lies that would identify the killers as 'reparations protesters' is a mockery to normal intelligence. They went to rob and kill. They did not know their victim. They randomly followed another person to the house. Now in this fantasy of ignorance we are asked to believe they discovered Miree was from a family once owning slaves and their brutal crimes were acts of historic vengeance.

These childish distortions of fact only serve to further alienate the greater society from blacks and to homogenize the race as ignorant, violent and dangerous. In spite of the consequences of such publications, the black community appears to do nothing to restore its reputation as an integral part of society.

Neely Fuller uses his blog, "The Black Code Files" to tell young blacks that if they're man enough to kill someone, be man enough to shoot it out with the police or kill themselves.

The theme appears to be consistent throughout predominately black communications; black victimization is the fault of the white community. Some speak of the need for blacks to solve their problems but the problem usually finds its roots among whites.

In response, black crime forces a profile to be established in the white mind. Many whites are not so kind about their opinions of black people and it must be painful to responsible, respectful blacks to be characterized by the worst element of their race. Worse yet, however, is that some of the criticisms, no matter how fierce in their presentation, bear the seeds of truth.

"Blacks have the highest STD (sexually transmitted disease," posted one man, "according to the Centers of Disease Control website. The information is of 2010. This is no lie... "69% of U.S. Blacks have Gonorrhea," for example. Holy crap, I would *never* date any woman who has been with a black man from the highest probability of getting an STD. *Never*!"

In reality, the Center for Disease Control reports that "In 2010, the overall rate among blacks in the United States was 1,167.5 cases per 100,000, a 4.0% increase from the 2009 rate of 1,122.2 cases per 100,000. The rate of chlamydia (Chlamydia is a sexually transmitted bacterial infection with symptoms similar to those of gonorrhea) among black women was over seven times the rate among white women (1,536.5 and 205.1 per 100,000 women, respectively. The chlamydia rate among black men was almost 11 times the rate among white men (761.8 and 69.9 cases per 100,000 men, respectively).

When asked for his opinion about racism in America, one USC professor asking to remain anonymous replied, "The new generations of blacks are angry people. Most of the time they need to find something to be angry about. By observing them over a long period of time, one begins to see the belief systems manipulating them. Black themed websites call for revolution, demand reparation for slavery inflicted upon past generations and defend every crime by claiming it was inspired by abuses by the white community.

"One must ask why blacks cannot celebrate the sacrifices of their forefathers who suffered in slavery because without them, they would be dying of hunger and AIDS in Africa today."

As black youth slips into the gangsta subculture, inspired by the negative messages found in rap and the acceptance of criminal rapsters as role models, too many black parents blame alleged failures by society instead of monitoring the influences. Can it be truly proven that rap and hip-hop lyrics do not contribute to delinquency? The explicit content of some hip-hop song lyrics, extolling violence and drug and alcohol use, detailing sexual exploits and gang adventures certainly relate to the activity of the gang culture. Various studies have shown a correlation between undesirable behaviors and lyrics describing or espousing violent, sexist or illegal activities. The American Academy of Pediatrics cites several studies as part of its 2009 "Impact of Music, Music Lyrics, and Music Videos on Children and Youth" report that shows a connection between violent lyrical and visual content and aggression, sexual content and sexual activity, sexist content and sexist attitudes. Some studies also show an increase in risk-taking behavior and drug use associated with certain music.

David Bender and Bruno Leone recommended that gangsta rap recordings should not be sold to minors a decade ago in their study, "Gangs: Opposing Viewpoints:"

"The lyrics and images contained in 'gangsta rap' performed predominantly by young blacks emulating gang members poisons the mind of inner-city youth and glamorizes and encourages crime, violence, vulgar language and the abuse of women: therefore, the sale of obscene gansta rap music to minors should be banned.

"The proliferation of violence and unacceptable sexual messages in young people's music is due in large part to the record industry's avarice. Approximately $780 million worth of rap records were sold in 1993, more than half the purchasers were under 17 years of age and 50 percent between 10 and 14 years of age. Lyrices in gangsta rap glorify violence and denigrate women. As a form of pornography, such music encourages youth to commit violent acts, use drugs, and abuse women through demeaning sex acts. The constant exposure of youth to negative images lowers their sensibilities toward violent behavior, making killing and abuse commonplace and acceptable. In addition to the proliferation of violent behavior, gangsta rap inculates in youth false and hateful concepts about women. Even if a direct link cannot be made between gangsta rap and violence, parents and elected officials need to be seriously concerned about the music because it is obscene and sexist, is driven by racism and greed, and ultimately destroys community values. Banning the sale of gangsta rap to children is one action government can take to curb youth violence."

In the decade following that publication, gangsta rap sales soared to new levels based on lyrics like:

"One 44, two 45's, 3 loaded clips, 4 niggas roll, one n*gga drives 500 Benz, 6 reasons why this kid should die," is heard in the works of the rapper Nas.

"Decapitatin I ain't hesitatin' to put you in the funeral home, with a bullet in your dome, I'm hot like lava, You got a problem? I've got a problem solver, and his name is revolver," is brought to children by Dr. Dre and Ice Cube.

Tupac raps, "Come take a journey through my mind's eye, You crossed the game, don't explain, n'gga time to die, say goodbye, watch my eyes when I pull the trigger, so right before you die you bow to a bigger n'ggar."

The profane, contaminating lyrics of rap are embraced by the gangsta culture and they become the anthems of their organized criminality. As early as 1988 a group calling itself "Fuck the Police" produced an album "Straight Outta Compton" with the lyrics:

Same fucking thing with the police / Cause the police just like fuckin' with people, you know / They stop you, throw you on the ground and shit / Put a gun to your head, and shit, you know what I'm saying / They just fuck with you for no reason / Anyway, fuck the police.

After this kind of introduction, it is no surprise that the rest of the song lives up to its name. Lyrics go as follows:

Fuck the police coming straight from the underground / A young nigger got it bad 'cause I'm brown / They have the authority to kill a minority / Fuck that shit cause I ain't the one / For a punk motherfucker with a badge and a gun to be beating on / Searching my car, looking for the product /Thinking every nigger is selling narcotas.

In 1993 Snoop Doggy Dogg brought respect for women to a new low with his "It Ain't No Fun."

Well if corrupt gave a fuck about a bitch, I'd always be broke / I'd never have no motherfuckin' en-do to smoke / I have no love for hoes, that's something that I learned in the past / So how am I supposed to pay this hoe /Just the latest hoe / I know the pussy's mine, so I'm gonna fuck a couple more times / And then I'm through wit' it / There's nothing else to do wit' it / Pass it to the homey, now you hit it / 'Cause she ain't nothing but a bitch to me and you all know / Bitches ain't shit to me / You'll never be my only one, trick ass bitch.

As vile as gangsta rap may be, it still finds its apologists such as black Thabiti Lewis who claims:

"Unfortunately what we do see in popular culture is the next phase of 1980s backlash politics aimed at demonizing Black males (single Black mothers too) – and their deficiencies. What is obscured is a history of American violence and a fascination with gangsta. Nor is much attention paid to the role of an increasingly violent American culture, rife with gangsters, guns, drugs, and social and economic policies that produced many of the ills the bad men get credit for creating. In popular sports and entertainment Black men often emerge as inherently visceral, irreverent, bad people without a cause. The popularization of hip-hop via a gangsta emphasis on violence, explicit sex, and drug use have blurred the unknowing eye from seeing hop-hip as the formidable force of peace and self expression that is its genesis."

According to this essay, if we cannot perceive that gangsta rap and hip-hop as a "force of peace," we are simply "unknowing." If we find the degradation of women offensive, we are out of the social loop. We are out of tune with the gangsta rap poison if we consider its "self expression" to be a sad commentary to the human condition.

Amal Saleeby Malek, PhD, also black, maintains that, "Rap music is the black community sharing their culture and telling their stories in their own special way."

Essentially, Malek is probably right but the culture and stories being told speak of violence, brutality toward women, the glorification of crime and a trend toward a race being accurately characterized by its offenses. And just as Lewis maintains that those opposing the negative influences of hip-hop and rap are "unknowing," Malek goes a step farther by stating, "Rap is certainly not understood by everyone. It is not a familiar art form, which may be one of the reasons it is feared and perceived as a threat. Thus, when rap is labeled as evil and as inciting violence, it is mostly ignorance that is at play."

We must then assume that the Colorado Springs, Colo. Police Department must be ignorant when the New York Times reported, "After a spate of shootings, and with a rising murder rate, the police here are saying gangsta rap is contributing to the violence, luring gang members and criminal activity to nightclubs. The police publicly condemned the music in a news release after a killing in July and are warning nightclub owners that their places might not be safe if they play gangsta rap.

"We don't want to broad-brush hip-hop music altogether," said Lt. Skip Arms, a police spokesman, "but we're looking at a subcomponent that typically glorifies, promotes criminal behavior and demeans women."

Colorado Springs police weren't the only ones dealing with the question of gangsta rap and street crime. The Baltimore Sun reported in 1994, "The debate over the social impact of gangsta rap music moves to a Milwaukee courtroom Wednesday, when two Wisconsin minors will be charged with murder in the country's second case of rap allegedly inspiring the killing of a police officer.

"The case involves two teens who told authorities they plotted a Sept. 7 sniper attack on a police van "because of a Tupac Shakur record that talks about killing the police." The assault resulted in the shooting death of 31-year-old Milwaukee Police Officer William A. Robertson."

The article included, "Assistant Dist. Atty. Mark Williams declined comment on the case, but sources in the Milwaukee County Homicide Unit said Shakur's violence-laced rap music will play a pivotal role in the prosecution's attempt to establish a motive for the first-degree "intentional" homicide.

"Walker, the alleged trigger man, told the police that Shakur's angry lyrics on South Central Cartel's album " 'N Gatz We Truss" "geeked him up" to stalk the officer, according to his court-appointed attorney Ann T. Bowe.

"'The violent anti-police lyrics appear to have acted as command hallucinations which influenced his behavior,' said Bowe, whose client has a six-year history of drug, burglary and weapons offenses. 'This young man insists that certain passages in these songs are so much a part of his consciousness that it was as if they just kept playing over and over in his head that night'"

Debbie Pelley's testimony before the U.S. Senate Commerce Committee, June 16, 1998 gives a graphic example of hip-hop and its influence.

"My name is Debbie Pelley. I am a teacher at Westside Middle School in Jonesboro, Arkansas and was present when four students and one teacher were killed and ten others injured by two 11- and 13-year-old boys as the students evacuated the school building when a false fire alarm sounded on March 24, 1998.

"1 was the English teacher for the 13-year-old, Mitchell Johnson, and had him in class an hour a day from August 15 to March 24. Mitchell was always respectful, using "yes ma'am" and "no ma'am" in his responses to me. In my class I never saw him exhibit anger, never saw him commit any hostile act toward any other student or exhibit any behavior that would make me think Mitchell could commit this act.

In fact, he had a pleasant and even cheerful disposition and appeared to enjoy his many friends, and to enjoy life in general. In a discussion with 7th grade classes the first day they were back at school after this tragedy, a discussion led by myself and another licensed professional counselor, James N. Woods, students explored possible reasons Mitchell could have committed this act. The students said that Mitchell had been listening to gangster rap music, and in particular to 'I'uPac Shakur. They also said he had started to change a lot in the last two or three months.

"On succeeding days numerous students on many occasions contributed the following information. TuPac Shakur and another rap group, Bone Thugs -N- Harmony, were Mitchell's favorite musical groups. (At this point I had never heard of either of these groups.) Mitchell brought this music to school with him; listened to it on the bus; tried listening to it in classes, sang the lyrics over and over at school, and played a cassette in the bathroom 'about coming to school and killing all the kids.' Students said that in the last couple of months Mitchell was always making the gang sign that is on the cover Of 'I'uPac's album, *All Eyez On Me*, and that Mitchell was far more into this music than anyone else they knew. Mitchell's mother, and Mitchell himself recently confirmed that he bought these albums this last Christmas, three months before the tragedy.

"One boy brought a CD by TuPac that Mitchell had lent to him and told me I could keep it, saying he didn't want to have anything more to do with the music because he felt it may have been an influence in Mitchell's life that led to this tragedy.

"These 12-year-old students showed me how to pull these lyrics by TuPac and Bone Thugs off the internet (about 500 pages of violent lyrics) and then identified Mitchell's favorite albums and songs that he was always singing. Following are a few examples of titles and quotes from those songs the way they are recorded on the internet. I wish every adult would take the time to read these lyrics as I have done. Most adults would be in for quite a shock.

"Crept and We Came" by Bone Thugs from the album, *Eternal E. 1999*: "Cockin the 9 and ready to aim/Pullin the Trigger/To blow Out Your brains/Bone got a gang/Man we crept and we came." (This song has about 40 murder images like "putten them in the ground and pumpin the gun." Mitchell's mother recently confirmed that Mitchell is still very familiar with the lyrics to this song. The last words of this song are quite revealing considering the way Mitchell and Drew killed the five and injured the ten so stealthily.)

"Body Rott" by Bone Thugs from the album, *Art of War: World War I*. One refrain used over and over in t[iis song is "Nigga the war shouldn't stop until these * cops' body rott, body rott." This song contains the "f" word 23 times and several references to bitches and hoes their usual expressions for females).

"Life Goes On" from the *All Eyez On Me* album by TuPac: "My homie from high school/he's getting by/It's time to bury another brotha/ nobody cry."

"I Ain't Mad At Ya" by TuPac from the *All Eyez On Me* album: "I can see us after school/we'd bomb on the first shit/With the wrong shit on."

"2 Of Amerikaz Most Wanted" bv TuPac from the album *All Eyez On Me*: Some fitting words since they killed and injured all females but one are these two lines: "Picture perfect, I paint a perfect picture/bomb the hoochies with precision." Then the refrain "Ain't nuttin but a gangsta party" is repeated five times in the chorus, and the chorus is repeated several times in the song.

"Shorty Wanna Be A Thug" by TuPac from the *All Eyez On Me* album: "He was a nice middle class nigga/But nobody knew the evil he'd do when he got a little bigger/. . . Was only sixteen, yet convicted as a felon/With a bunch of old niggas." Chorus, "Say he wanna be/Shorties gonna be a Thug/Said he wanna be/One day he's gonna be/Said he's gonna be/Shorties gonna be's a thug." (Last part is repeated several times in each chorus.)

"Bury Me A G" bv TuPac from the *Thug Life Vol. I* album: "I got nothen' to lose sos I choose to be a killer/Went from bangin' to slangin/Now I'm a dope dealer/All my a paid tha price to be the boss/Back in school/Wrote tha rules on gettin' tossed/Popping rocks on the block was a past time/Pack a 9 all the time."

"Blaze It" by Bone Thugs from the album *The Art of War: World War II*: "I'm so high/If reefer really makes you happy, nigga blaze it/Hell yeah, Bell yeah/Stay smokin', chokin', /Rollin' blunts and we love it/We smoke and choke/We smoke and choke, and we love it. (This is repeated several times.) "Now, I've been fucked up since the last weed song/and P.O.D.'d the whole night long."

"Several students verified that the theme and message of this music is that killing and being on death row are cool. The students themselves pointed out that the recording company that publishes TuPac is called Death Row Records and showed me that on the *All Eyez On Me* album the cover advertises upcoming Death Row releases and one of them is called *Death Row Compilation*. One of the songs by Bone Thugs -N- Harmony, "If I Could Teach the World" from the album *The Art Of War: World War I* says, 'If I could teach the world, Then I would teach the world, whole wide world to be a thugsta just like me, like.' That seems to be the point of their music.

"On June 1, 1998 Mitchell Johnson's mother said that Mitchell himself said that the music may have influenced him and that the music sort of draws you in. She confirmed to me that Mitch did possess, and she still has, Mitchell's albums and cassettes by TuPac and by Bone Thugs. She knew he bought them this last Christmas before the shooting in March with money he had received as a Christmas present from relatives.

"Mitchell told her he bought them himself and had no trouble purchasing them. As noted above, numerous students reported the first day back at school that Mitch had started to change a lot the last two or three months and was making gang signs in the hall and around school.

"Mitch's mother said he had always loved music and had sung specials at church and school since he was very little and that he owned and sang western music and gospel music as well. She did not know Mitchell had any that had warning labels on it. (These warning labels are in very small print and barely legible.) When she questioned Mitchell recently, he said he was first exposed to rap music through a girl in the neighborhood in Minnesota who had TuPac's music. He said he liked it because it was different. That was two years ago, when Mitchell and the girl were both 11 years old."

"I believe," she continued, "the message coming out of the tragedy in our school in Jonesboro, Arkansas is that even the good schools and responsible families can no longer protect their children from our society. Violent music is only one aspect of our culture but a very significant one that seems to have gotten very little attention in the recent school tragedies, and Bone Thugs and TuPac are only two of the many musical groups that are affecting our youth. According to the *Pittsburgh Post Gazette*, [on] May 22, 1998 Andrew Wurst, the 14-year-old boy who shot a teacher and injured two others in Edinboro, Pennsylvania, 'called himself Satan and liked the rock group Marilyn Manson.'

"I believe that legislators who are elected to represent and protect the citizens in our country should find a way to investigate the scope of this problem, to protect our children from this music, and to educate the parents and society even as I have been educated in the last several weeks."

Dr. Craig A. Anderson summarized a study by the American Psychological Association on the influence of rap music on young people with, ""One major conclusion from this and other research on violent entertainment media is that content matters," said Dr. Anderson. "This message is important for all consumers, but especially for parents of children and adolescents."

One may ask if the impact of violent music can be distinguished from the lives of the rappers themselves. No less than 66 prominent rappers have jail or prison records and an encyclopedia of criminal offenses. Perhaps Malik is correct is saying that rappers tell the stories of their lives and we can see it when reviewing that Scot La Rock was shot to death at the age of 25. King Tubby was 58 when he was murdered. Double Trouble was soaked in gasoline and set on fire at the age of 29. MC Rock was stabbed to death when he was 28.

Rappers Brandon Mitchell, The Mac, Charizma, Mr. Cee, Ricky Herd, Tupac Shakur, Yaki Kadafi, Seagram Miller, Notorious B.I.G., Jo Jo White, Fat Pat, Malcolm Howard, MC Big L , Rapper MC Ant, Dion Stewart, Karnail Pitts, Freaky Tah, Q-Don, Johnny Burns, Bruce Mayfield, Erik Carson, Lloyd "Mooseman" Roberts, Jam

Master Jay, Freako, Holy Quran, Dr. Dre, Anthony Watkins, Deshaun Holton, Big Hawk and Stack Bundles were all shot to death.

Easy-E died of AIDS at 31. Rapper Young Lay was shot but survived only to have his baby kidnapped and his girlfriend die in a house fire that was determined to be arson. Tonnie Sheppard was stabbed to death in a recording studio and the list goes on.

Rap and hip-hop, glorified by the apologists as mere cultural expressions are the product of rappers who not only promote violence and brutal behavior but also live it. It could be legitimately claimed that those defending this form of music could be as negatively affected by it as those who blame it for inspiring them to commit heinous crimes.

Ronald Ray Howard was driving a stolen car in July of 1992 when Texas Highway Patrolman Bill Davidson pulled him over for having a broken headlight. Howard had the radio on listening to Tupac Shakur's 'Soulja's Story' that tells the sob story of a young thug who is pulled over and then shoots the policeman. He told the court that he was inspired to kill Davidson by the song and related the impact that gangsta rap had on his life. He was found guilty and later executed.

To even suggest that young, impressionable minds cannot be influenced by the rhythmic offerings of rap with all its glorification of cop killing, ho domination and the imagery of the thug being the supreme defense of his race is ludicrous at least.

To then have the worst of his actions justified in black themed websites bearing no relationship to truth or reality gives assurance that his defiance and delinquency are not his responsibility, rather the consequence of an unfair and oppressive society.

At the same time, little is said or done about black parenting that far too often contributes to the delinquency of their children. Street life in the late hours can never be considered a wholesome environment and yet it is found in case records across the land.

The modern black image is still in the process of formation but the implications are clear. Black youth is molding the shape of their race into the characterization of crime, danger, death, violence, threat, disrespect, hatred and an organized effort to justify it all through an assortment of misrepresentations and lies.

When an independent poll asked black youth in New York's Harlem about what makes them so angry, one answered, "Whitey took my people from their homes and now we can never go back.

Whenever I hear anyone arguing for slavery,
I feel a strong impulse to see it tried on him personally.
Abraham Lincoln

THE AFRICAN EXPERIENCE

It would be a good lesson for black leaders to pretend for a while that Abraham Lincoln had not been assassinated and that the plans for post-war America in 1865 had been completed.

In his debates with Stephen Douglas, Lincoln stated, ""I will say, then, that I am not, nor ever have been, in favor of bringing about in any way the social and political equality of the white and black races: that I am not, nor ever have been, in favor of making voters or jurors of negroes, nor of qualifying them to hold office, nor to intermarry with white people."

In the presidential election of 1860, after counting the ballots from Alabama, Arkansas, Florida, Georgia, North Carolina, Louisiana, Tennessee, South Carolina and Texas, Abraham Lincoln had a total of 0 votes. Slaves states opposed the concept of emancipation. To the Southern mentality it was taking away their property as surely as if they had burned their crops or tore down their homes.

In that year, 1860, nearly a half million free blacks lived in the Northern states and 3,953,760 slaves lived in the Southern states. It wasn't a simple matter of one day saying, "Okay, you're all free now."

Where would nearly four million ex-slaves go? What would they do? Where would they live? They were not prepared to do anything other than work in the fields or be house servants. They had no education that would enable them to find other forms of labor.

Others simply didn't care. The belief that the black slave was less than human continued in the minds of many. After all, only a few years before Charles Darwin had said:

"Since the dawn of history the Negro has owned the continent of Africa - rich beyond the dream of poet's fancy, crunching acres of diamonds beneath his bare black feet and yet he never picked one up from the dust until a white man showed to him its glittering light.

"His land swarmed with powerful and docile anmals, yet he never dreamed a harness, cart, or sled.

"A hunter by necessity, he never made an axe, spear, or arrowhead worth preserving beyond the moment of its use. He lived as an ox, content to graze for an hour.

"In a land of stone and timber he never sawed a foot of lumber, carved a block, or built a house save of broken sticks and mud.

"With league on league of ocean strand and miles of inland seas, for four thousand years he watched their surface ripple under the wind, heard the thunder of the surf on his beach, the howl of the storm over his head, gazed on the dim blue horizon calling him to worlds that lie beyond, and yet he never dreamed a sail."

The Supreme Court, after all, had practically said that black slaves were not human, rather they were the property of their owners.

In March of 1857, the United States Supreme Court, led by Chief Justice Roger B. Taney, declared that all blacks -- slaves as well as free -- were not and could never become citizens of the United States. The court also declared the 1820 Missouri Compromise unconstitutional, thus permiting slavery in all of the country's territories.

The case before the court was that of *Dred Scott v. Sanford.* Dred Scott, a slave who had lived in the free state of Illinois and the free territory of Wisconsin before moving back to the slave state of Missouri, had appealed to the Supreme Court in hopes of being granted his freedom.

Taney, a staunch supporter of slavery and intent on protecting southerners from northern aggression, wrote in the Court's majority opinion that, because Scott was black, he was not a citizen and therefore had no right to sue. The framers of the Constitution, he wrote, believed that blacks "had no rights which the white man was bound to respect; and that the negro might justly and lawfully be reduced to slavery for his benefit. He was bought and sold and treated as an ordinary article of merchandise and traffic, whenever profit could be made by it."

Referring to the language in the Declaration of Independence that includes the phrase, "all men are created equal," Taney reasoned that "it is too clear for dispute, that the enslaved African race were not intended to be included, and formed no part of the people who framed and adopted this declaration. . . ."

America had a long history of viewing black slaves as "things" rather than human beings. Thomas Jefferson, a slave owner himself, said, "I advanced it, therefore, as a suspicion only, that the blacks, whether originally a distinct race or made distinct by time or circumstance, are inferior to the whites in the endowments of both body and mind."

The great philosopher, David Hume, had stated, "I am apt to suspect the Negroes...to be naturally inferior to the White. There never was a civilized nation of any other complexion than white, nor even any individual eminent either in action or speculation, not ingenious manufacturers amongst them, not arts, or sciences."

The common thought of the day was that slave traders had gone to Africa and taken from the jungles man-like creatures that could be taught to work.

It would be a mistake to believe that the tragedy of slavery belonged only to black people. Slaves once served in the Vatican and since it was a Papal order that Christians could not be enslaved, the Christianized natives of Paraguay were put in chains after being determined "non-human" and taken to serve in the homes and fields of Spain and Portugal.

The galley ships of the Papal States were rowed by slaves and it was not until diseases brought by the Spanish Conquistadors to the New World had diminished the native population drastically that Bishop Las Casas authorized the first boat load of African slaves to be brought to the West Indies. As late as the 1820s, Capuchin missionaries in the U.S. protesting black slavery were excommunicated.

In 1866, after the emancipation of slaves in the United States, Pope Pius IX declared that it was not against divine law for someone to sell, buy or exchange a slave.

There is a tendency in America for young people to believe that white colonists suddenly decided to go to Africa and capture people there to use as slaves. That is far from the truth. The slave trade of a three hundred year period was equal to the drug trade of today. It was big business and slavery was embraced by most of the western world.

Colombia was one of the major ports for the entry of slave ships from Africa. Slaves were also taken to Ecuador, Peru, Costa Rica, Panama and Brazil.

African slaves worked in the mines of Bolivia; a labor far more difficult and dangerous than any known in the United States. Mules were used to push the mills in the royal mint but only survived this hard labor an average of two months. Using African slaves to push the miles was considered to be more "cost effective."

When the French constructed a railroad across Panama to link the Atlantic and Pacific Oceans, it was done with black slave labor. They later attempted to construct a canal but the project was abandoned in 1893 because of the high death toll of the workers. Moderate estimates tell of 22,000 deaths in the failed canal project, most descendants of African slaves.

Slavery throughout western Europe and the Americas gave a collective view of the black slave as a creature used to work rather than a human longing for freedom.

Now to consider the idea of liberating all the slaves brought special, fearful problems. The flood of free blacks would be a nuisance to a progressive society. Politicians busied themselves with not trying to find ways to fit former slaves into society, rather to merely find a way for them to survive. They would later try to do the same for the western buffalo and both were done with the same amount of compassion. While the Great Emancipator never envisioned that blacks would be equal to white citizens and while he opposed the idea of slavery, he was not especially considerate of those who were actually enslaved and established a plan to ship them to Guyana, Haiti and Liberia.

"Negro Equality! Fudge!" he exclaimed during his famed debates. "How long in the government of a God great enough to make and maintain this Universe shall there continue knaves to vend and fools to gulp so low a piece of demagoguism as this?

"Judge Douglas has said to you that he has not been able to get from me an answer to the question whether I am in favor of negro citizenship. So far as I know, the Judge never asked me the question before. He shall have no occasion to ever ask it again, for I tell him very frankly that I am not in favor of negro citizenship".

"I am not, nor ever have been in favor of bringing about in any way the social and political equality of the white and black races, that I am not nor ever have been in favor of making voters or jurers of negroes, nor of qualifying them to hold office, not to intermarry with White people; There is a physical difference between the White and black races which I believe will forever forbid the two races living together on equal terms of social and political equality. And inasmuch as they cannot so live, while they do remain together there must be the position of superior and inferior, and I as much as any other man am in favor of having the superior position assigned to the White race."

When England abolished the slave trade in 1772, an effort was made to resettle slaves back to their native Africa. The program began with 300 former slaves and 70 white prostitutes being sent to the Sierra Leone peninsula in West Africa. It didn't take long for disease and warfare with a local tribe to take their toll and the project was considered a failure.

Another attempt was made in 1792 with 1,100 freed slaves were taken to the newly established Freetown in Sierra Leone. By 1820, emancipated slaves from the United States arrived at the colony. A year later the American Colonization Society established a colony called Liberia that became the nation known today. Its capitol is called Monrovia in honor of James Monroe who assisted greatly in its founding.

Between 1821 and 1860, about 15,000 ex-slaves settled in Liberia and established its government and became independent in 1847.

In 2009, an order from Lincoln was discovered in the Archives of Pew in England authorizing a British colonial agent, John Hodge, to recruit freed slaves to be relocated to areas that are now Guyana and Belize.

"Hodge reported back to a British minister that Lincoln said it was his 'honest desire' that this emigration went ahead."

The plan came despite an earlier test shipment of about 450 freed slaves to Haiti resulting in disaster. The former slaves were struck by smallpox and starvation, and survivors had to be rescued.

Mr Lincoln also considered sending freed slaves to what is now Panama, to construct a canal — decades before work began on the modern canal there in 1904.

The colonization plan collapsed by 1864. The British were fearful the confederate states of the American south may win the civil war, reverse emancipation, and regard British agents as thieves. Congress also voted to remove funding.

Yet as late as that autumn, a letter sent to the president by his attorney-general showed he was still actively exploring whether the policy could be implemented, Mr Page said.

"It says 'further to your question, yes, I think you can still pursue this policy of colonization even though the money has been taken away'," he said.

The plan was not new. On October 15, 1854, Lincoln told an audience in Peoria, Illinois:

"My first impulse would be to free all the slaves, and send them to Liberia, to their own native land. But a moment's reflection would convince me that whatever of high hope (as I think there is) there may be in this, in the long run, its sudden execution is impossible."

In his State of the Union address of 1861, he again mentioned the issue:

"You [blacks] and we [whites] are of different races. This physical difference is a great disadvantage to both of us. Your race is suffering, in my opinion, one of the most grievous injustices inflicted on any people. But, even when you are freed from slavery, you are far from equal with the white race. That is why it is better for both races to be kept separate."

Historic documents serve to indicate that Lincoln was persistent in his desire to relocate former slaves out of the United States. Lincoln was, after all, a member of the

American Colonial Society that had established the colony in Liberia. When the former slaves decided to declare Liberia independent, however, politicians in the U.S. were not happy. The nation, under President James Polk, was too busy, however, conducting its war of expansion against Mexico to do much about it.

The situation had changed by 1865. Lincoln had encouraged men mustering out of the Union Army to go to Mexico and help that nation and Benito Juarez in their struggle against France. He might have been trying to score points with Juarez for a different reason.

In 1861, Lincoln had sent Montgomery Blair, Post Master General to meet with Matias Romero, Charge d'Affaires de Mexico in Washington, D.C.

Blair and Romero had established a friendship over the years and Lincoln thought it might be exploited. Romero later stated that Blair had told him:

"Cozumel is a deserted island which in no way serves the Mexicans, and the white race could not possibly acclimatize itself on Cozumel or Yucatan, which is inhabited by Indians. These regions are destined to be populated by Negroes. We need to rid ourselves of them, and we could not encounter another place more appropriate to send them than that island."

Romero also stated that he later met with Secretary of State William Henry Seward and finally told him that the purchase of Cozumel would be "impossible." The people of Mexico were not willing to lose another inch of their territory to the United States at any price. Mexico would, however, consider accepting "certain, selected, freed slaves" as immigrants.

Many in Washington were certain that the Cozumel purchase was a sure thing and the head of the Senate Foreign Relations Committee, Senator James Rand Doolittle, spearheaded a bill authorizing Lincoln to purchase a foreign territory and used his influence to push it through an easy vote.

Blair was pleased that the measure passed, saying that he was eager to send freed slaves to ". . . the hot lands of Southern Mexico where they could do the agricultural labor for which they were deemed suitable."

Not long after it became known to all that Mexico was not interested in selling Cozumel and it was obvious a new strategy was needed.

In mid-May of 1862, Robert Wilson Shufeldt, U.S. Consul General to Cuba, met with Manuel Doblado, Mexico's Minister of Foreign Relations, to present yet another of Lincoln's plans. This time the U.S. would send its liberated slaves to the Isthmus of Tehuantepec. The United States had been trying to negotiate with Mexico to buy that property since the 1840s with little luck and now it seemed a good alternative to propose it to be a black resettlement colony.

Originally, U.S. interest in Tehuantepec had been to build a road and railroad that would connect the Atlantic to the Pacific Ocean as a earlier vision of the Panama Canal.

Soon thereafter, Mexico rejected this idea as well.

At that time, a wealthy American, Ambrose W. Thompson, owned a large tract of land in the Chiriqui Province of Panama. With the rejection of Mexico, the next plan was to utilize Thompson's land and relocate 50,000 of the freed slaves to Panama.

Hearing of the plan, the Governments of Guatemala and Nicaragua protested that such a project should be planned so close to their borders and soon after the plan was abandoned.

Later that year, 500 freed slaves were sent to Ille a Vache on the coast of Haiti. As predicted by some of the critics, however, a military expedition had to be sent there to prevent them from starving to death.

Lincoln had to face the fact that his project of relocating freed slaves outside of the United States was not going to be successful. The last alternative was all that was left to him; the freed slaves would have to live in the United States.

If we turn back the clock enough and imagine that the relocation plan had been successful, where would today's black youth live?

Liberia is now a nation of 1.2 million people where two babies are dying every hour and where one in nine children do not reach their fifth birthday. One in 12 women does not survive childbirth and instead of seeking professional medical care, most find their remedies among witch doctors.

The nation suffered a long and bloody civil war and its ex-president, Charles Taylor, is in England serving the final 30 years of his sentence. He was convicted of war crimes and crimes against humanity relating to his role in aiding murderous rebels who committed atrocities in Sierra Leone, one of Liberia's northern neighbors, during its civil war in the 1990s.

He was accused of fomenting widespread brutality that included murder, rape, the use of child soldiers, the mutilation of thousands of civilians and the mining of diamonds to pay for guns and ammunition.

Liberia's capital, Monrovia, is home to a third of the nation's population, often without resources and installations such as water and sanitation facilities.

Widespread malnutrition was reported throughout the country and special projects were enacted to reduce morbidity and mortality from malnutrition in children under five years old in Greater Monrovia.

Haiti, Guyana, Cuba – almost every site that was once considered as a place to relocate freed slaves in the 1860s is today impoverished, disease ridden and disadvantaged.

With the publication of the Alex Haley novel *Roots* in 1976, there was a minor movement of blacks wanting to return to Africa and re-establish the heritage lost to slavery. Organizations exist yet today to assist families wanting to expatriate to Africa. The stories coming out of these efforts, however, are less than enticing to others. Culture shock, overwhelming poverty and ignorance, disease and the lack of modern technology all usually make the repatriation a sad and tormented experience.

Had the repatriation programs of Lincoln been successful, there can be no question that the modern black would live in conditions far worse than those known in the United States. Perhaps this is not a fair comparison since it does not address the reality of today's situation, but historically it has considerable merit. More significant is that today's black leaders have never addressed this subject or attempted to find a more positive viewpoint to modern conditions.

As offensive as it may be to some, the same can be said about slavery itself. The modern American black would be faced with a much more difficult life and struggle for survival had slavery never taken place. The same regions of Africa where most of the slaves were taken are now plagued with starvation, disease, civil wars and extreme poverty.

That does not mean that the modern black should be thankful that slavery is part of their collective history, rather that the hardships and sacrifices of their forefathers should be respected and honored.

Modern youth making comments that their forefathers were taken from their homes and "we can never go back," do not appreciate the advantages they enjoy over black youth living in Africa. The benefits they so willingly reject would be treasured by most of their African peers. A free education, efficient medical care, social programs and a host of resources are available if they choose to accept them.

American blacks have a nation unemployment rate of 12.6% as compared to Sub-Sahara Africa's 51% for young black women and 43% of young men who are chronically unemployed.

For a modern black youth in America to lament that "we can never go back" merely evidences a lack of knowledge.

Never doubt that a small group of thoughtful,
concerned citizens can change world.
Indeed it is the only thing that ever has.
Margaret Mead

FANTASIES AND FALLACIES

If the statistics relating to crimes committed by young black youth dealt with a disease instead of criminal offenses, it would be called an epidemic. Like any epidemic, the problem is growing. As far back as 2008, 83% of all armed assailants in New York City were black even though blacks represented only 24% of the population. When combined with Hispanics, blacks were responsible for 98% of all assaults involving a gun. Forty-nine of 50 muggings were committed by blacks or Hispanics.

Ray Kelly, New York City Police Commissioner verifies the statistics stating that 96% of all crimes were committed by blacks or Hispanics.

FBI statistics for that time period reveal that blacks committed 433,934 crimes against whites as compared to the 55,685 of whites against blacks. Blacks were eight times more likely to assault a white person than the reverse. In 2007, slightly more than 14,000 white women were raped by black men while the FBI statistics reported not one white man raped a black woman.

And if the FBI stats for 2007 represent an average year since the Tawana Brawley rape-hoax of 1987, over one-third of a million white women have been sexually assaulted by black males since 1987 — with no visible protest from the civil rights leadership.

Today, 73 percent of all black kids are born out of wedlock. Growing up, these kids drop out, use drugs, are unemployed, commit crimes and are incarcerated at many times the rate of Asians and whites.

The numbers makes it easy to stereotype blacks into a race of dangerous disorder and a willingness to be unproductive. But black children are taught the history of their race from the beginning of the black experience in America, not in Africa or its myriad of tribes. The consequence is that they believe their beginnings was found in chains, stolen from the dark continent to serve in the white man's world. The only value blacks had as individuals was how well they could serve others. For generations their talents and dreams held no importance and were stifled beneath the yoke of slavery.

There is a singularity to the teaching, suggesting that only blacks knew slavery or that it somehow represents an enduring debt remaining unpaid by the white world.

In spite of the bitterness lingering from the era of black slavery, modern blacks continue to mimic the speech patterns of their forefather slaves. The street black vernacular of "Doan axe me what he do," is reminiscent of the "Yah suh, massa."

The wildfire spread of street English among blacks could not be reversed and some school districts like Oakland, California passed resolutions to recognize the legitimacy of African American Vernacular English as a language. Bill Cosby thought differently, saying, "People marched and were hit in the face with rocks to get an education, and now we've got these knuckleheads walking around. They're standing on the corner and they can't speak English. I can't even talk the way these people talk....You can't be a doctor with that kind of crap coming out of your mouth. In fact you will never get any kind of job making a decent living."

Even so, in spite of the support of language experts and those viewing the decision of school boards as progressive, it largely represented a surrender to the fact that many black kids were not going to learn correct English and had no interest in trying.

There were suggestions that black youths did not want the white man's education even though they had no alternatives other than the street life that created the vernacular in the first place. Their minds were on pause in the era of their great-great grandfather, protesting the white mentality that produced slavery. They did not need the teaching of white men to know that their race had been wronged.

They knew nothing of Africa and had never stood on the auction block to be sold. They had no knowledge of plantation life or field work. They knew nothing of selective mating to produce bigger, stronger workers or of the wholesale social disorder after liberation. They only knew the word "slave" and made it the theme of their rebellion.

But the rebellion has not substance other than in the defiant mind. There are no new organizations or movements addressing the issues young blacks believe exist. It is sufficient to simply be angry and criminally violent by inventing the idea that nothing can be done until the white man lifts his foot from black necks. There are the imaginary protest movements with "black foot soldiers" and promises of a black revolution inspired by a supreme power that will send whites to hell.

There is no redemption for the whites who marched in the protest rallies for civil rights or the white members of Congress voting to enforce them. Whites are homogenized into the enemy and kept there because without being educated, how could they know about whites who shared the dream of equality and sacrificed for it?

There remains, however, that ever lingering connection that cannot be dismissed but always abhorred. Black women buy their hair straightener imitating Tyra Banks, Halle Berry, Beyonce Knowles, Oprah Winfrey, and Kelly Rowland. Black women often accept the white standard of defining beauty and try to be part of it and all the while subscribe to the logo that Black is Beautiful.

In some studies black men have expressed a preference for white women but that demands exploration. Is that preference legitimate or a mere extension of the ongoing protest? During most of the black experience in America, black men were prohibited to fraternize in any way with a white woman. Some were hanged for only looking at a white woman while white masters sometimes had sex with slave women. Without a definitive study it is difficult to say what motives cause the claimed preference but it might well be reduced to only, "Look at me now."

The stress and conflict of young blacks is, in many ways, shared by conforming black adults. There is the haunting awareness that they must be "good black people" or they will be judged with those who are not. They must speak properly, act correctly, make good decisions and have a good work record and learn to mix well. In many cases it is a matter of pretending every day or else they will be pigeon holed into the axiom that all blacks are the same.

Using correct English is known in the black community as "talking white." Having one's conduct proper and socially acceptable is "acting white." It is not the concept of what is right, rather what is white. It is not a matter of doing what is universally acceptable by standards of social behavior established centuries ago, it is a way of life dictated by the white world.

Within the framework of the black mindset is the idea that their image was not self-created by collective behavior but is the demeaning vision held by the white world. Whites do not want blacks to progress so they promote the image of blacks being loud, ugly, vulgar, ignorant, angry, domineering, lustful and sexually irresponsible, lazy, a thief, bullies, liars, murderers and rapists. Statistics proving that young blacks contaminate the image of the race as a whole is ignored and yet another product of the manipulating white man.

The clandestine message of the black underground is that race alone justifies and forgives the bitterness, rage, pride, jealousies and corrupted speech. Any act of a white man offending the nature of the black world is subject to physical vengeance that is, after all, understandable by underprivileged blacks. His world, he believes, has always been kept in the shadows of humanity and identified with the negativism of being black; black cat, black magic, black market, black list, black mark, black deed, black eye and on and on.

The blacks must invent derogatory names for whites like glacier monkey, honky, cracker, to retaliate for decades of being called niggers, coons or jungle bunnies. To emphasize the protest, black youths will call each other nigger but not permit it to be said by others without retaliating with physical violence.

Society must, however, ignore the litany of crimes black youth commit and the consequences forced upon respectable members of the black race. To be followed by store security, stopped by police, frisked and questioned all stem from a long and growing history of crime and violence that makes each black his own enemy and is helpless to do anything other than be resentful.

Part of the resentment of the hard working, responsible black citizen is that he is the specimen being judged as the species. He does not steal, kill or rape and yet he is feared on the street at night. A common belief is that he is part of the collective image and nothing about him is unique or special. He longs to be himself, apart from the racial image and yet his son believes the opposite. Blacks must be alike, amalgamated into the anger, bitterness and retaliations.

All the while the white community, through numbers and power alone, move forward and view the black protest as symbolic of ignorance and an allegiance to crime that has become almost an inheritance from one generation to the next. The white man does, however, have serious questions and resentment. Dr. Samuel Rutman of Cullman Research explains it as, "Show me one black kid who can tell you who William Lewis Moore was. He was a white postman from Baltimore, shot and killed during a one-man march against segregation. He had planned to deliver a letter to the governor of Mississippi urging an end to intolerance.

"Show me a black kid who knows anything about Rev. Bruce Klunder, a white civil rights activist who protested the building of a segregated school by placing his body in the way of construction equipment. He was crushed to death when a bulldozer backed over him.

"What black kid knows anything about Andrew Goodman and Michael Henry Schwerner, young white civil rights workers who were arrested by a deputy sheriff and then released into the hands of Klansmen who plotted their murders. They were killed for supporting the civil rights of blacks everywhere,

"Or how about Rev. James Reeb, the white minister from Boston, who joined the Selma marchers after the attack by state troopers at the Edmund Pettus Bridge. Reeb was beaten to death while he walked down a Selma street. And Viola Gregg Liuzzo, the white housewife and mother from Detroit, drove alone to Alabama to help with the Selma march after seeing televised reports of the attack at the Edmund Pettus Bridge. She was driving marchers back to Selma from Montgomery when she was shot and killed by a Klansmen in a passing car.

"So in the end, many whites died alongside blacks because they believed in the same cause. Other white people marched and donated and protested and thought it was worth it that black kids could study in schools with whites and learn to be friends. Hollywood had never given an Oscar to a black in those days and now it's a regular thing. It was all worth it, or so they thought.

"Now I am asked to donate to the United Negro College Fund that supports a long list of black colleges or watch the Black Entertainment Television. Blacks would be the first to protest the creation of a White Entertainment Television or the existence of an all-white college. In 1978, Allan Bakke, had to go to the Supreme Court to protest that he was twice refused entrance into Medical School because the university had to meet a quota of minority entrants under affirmative action rules. It was unfair. Grades, entrance exams or perseverance were unimportant, he wasn't admitted because the school had to admit black students with lower grades and exam scores.

"A 2009 Pew Poll revealed that the majority of Americans still supported affirmative action but only 22% of whites thought there should be racial preferences while 58% of blacks wanted the unfair practice to be continued. Black kids are wanting to play the victim card and get a free ride while offering absolutely nothing to society."

Among the few black leaders seriously addressing the problem of black youth is Phillip Jackson, Executive Director of The Black Star Project. Jackson has called for a program that would;

> 1) Teach all Black boys to read at grade level by the third grade and to embrace education.
>
> 2) Provide positive role models for Black boys.
>
> 3) Create a stable home environment for Black boys that includes contact with their fathers.

4)   Ensure that Black boys have a strong spiritual base.

5)   Control the negative media influences on Black boys.

6)   Teach Black boys to respect all girls and women.

Whether or not the goals will ever be accomplished, they do represent an awareness of the weaknesses within the community of black youth.

One must respect Jackson's honesty as he addresses the problems without assigning them as being inflicted by white men.

"Black men in prison in America have become as American as apple pie," says Jackson. "There are more black men in prisons and jails in the United States (about 1.1 million) than there are black men incarcerated in the rest of the world combined. This criminalization process now starts in elementary schools with black male children as young as six and seven years old being arrested in staggering numbers according to a 2005 report, Education on Lockdown by the Advancement Project."

Jackson correctly identifies the problem as the "criminalization process" rather than the NAACP cover up policies of attacking the criminal system. Jackson asked the critical questions, "America has lost a generation of black boys. Who are young black women going to marry? Who is going to build and maintain the economies of black communities? Where is the outrage of the black community at the destruction of its black boys?"

It is a detriment to the black image that an international protest could be organized to protest the death of Trayvon Martin but nothing can be done to save millions of others like him. Critics maintain that the Martin protest was simply a money making exercise formed by black lawyers and promoters. Sabrina Fulton, Trayvon's mother, joined a speakers bureau and was booked to speak at the University of Connecticut, Harvard Law School, the University of Utah and other locations, all for a fee. Critics felt her dedication to the cause of turning personal tragedy into an advocacy should be done through dedication, not deposits.

Jackson legitimately asked where was black leadership in this time of racial crisis? To conform to the gangsta culture of black youth, raster Kanye West has claimed that his accomplishments are greater than those of Nelson Mandela and he will take Mandela's place as the black leader. But where were the real leaders, not the unqualified pretenders? The black community always had leaders to present and defend their cause. Sojourner Truth, Harriet Tubman and Frederick Douglass during the abolitionist era or Ida B. Wells, Booker T. Washington and W.E.B DuBois protesting racism at the turn of the 20th century.

As that century passed its halfway point, there began a separation within the black community. The 70s and 80s found drugs entering the inner cities and as legal issues threatened to dilute the civil rights achieved a decade before, black leaders decided that protest was more important than leadership. There was no effort to analyze or be self-critical; leaders thought protest was a sign of unity and force.

The back stabbing and in-fighting not only divided the sense of leadership but separated blacks into a near caste system as upwardly mobile blacks sought the suburbs and the poor blacks settled into the tenements and projects. The very freedoms black sought were now forming chasms between them as life before in segregated communities bound them in unity and a singularity of cause. Now the professional and poor were moving apart into different worlds. Today's black middle class of working professionals believe they are living in the post-racial time of America while the impoverished in the projects believe it has never truly ended. Somewhere between or below these two factions dwell today's black youth recognizing the importance that the nation finally has a black president but totally unaware that David Dinkins was the black Mayor of New York City or that Douglas Wilder was elected as the first black governor of Virginia since the Reconstruction years. The only message is one of hatred for whites as black websites cry for reparation for the slavery years as if to say, "It's not just protesting a wrong, I also want to profit from it."

At times, whatever black leadership there really is fades into obscurity in the midst of true social opportunity. Blacks did not support the Occupy Wall Street movement. Unemployment among blacks was about seven percent higher than whites. In the half decade before the Occupy Movement, black households had lost 52% of their median net worth but blacks, representing about 12% of the nation's population, represented only 1.6% of the people involved in the movement. Black leaders were equally absent and only Cornel West, Russell Simmons, Kanye West and Rep. John Lewis of Georgia made appearances in support.

Many of the Occupier's issues of protest were like those long known to blacks and still they did not come. Was it because there was nothing in it for black leaders? It was well known that as early as the 1980s, black leaders had been in bed with the tobacco and alcohol companies. The NAACP, United Negro College Fund and the Congressional Black Caucus all had big time donations from the tobacco and alcohol industries without regard to the general health of blacks. AT&T and Comcast were doling out money to the Congressional Black Caucus and other civil rights groups and it was not important that these were the firms opposing universal access to the internet. In other words, why should blacks participate in the Occupy Movement against the oppressive corporate machine when their own leaders were part of it?

The supposed idealism of young blacks certainly wasn't backed by their hip-hop idols either. None of them have spoken out about issues like police brutality, poverty, disenfranchisement or disadvantage. None appeared at any of the Occupy sites but Jay-Z thought it was okay to capitalize on the movement to produce "Occupy All Streets" T-shirts and sell them for $22 each and not donate a dime to the movement. Like the misguided reparations topic, it all operates on the theme, "What's in it for me?"

A poll was commissioned by Black Entertainment Television founder Robert L. Johnson and released by Zogby Analytics. According to the online survey of 1,002 African-Americans, when asked the question "Which of the following speaks for you most often?" 40 percent said that no one speaks for them, while 24 percent said the Reverend Al Sharpton of the National Action Network and MSNBC speaks for black people, and 11 percent said the Reverend Jesse Jackson of Rainbow PUSH.

"My primary concern is why, after enacting and enforcing needed civil and equal rights laws, spending more money on education for African-American students at all levels than at any other time in the history of this nation, and having twice elected an African-American president, black American families are still experiencing a growing disparity in employment, access to capital, wealth accumulation, and as a direct consequence, stagnation in economic opportunity and quality of life," Johnson said of the poll.

In the age of Barak Obama, a black president is not enough for the black community. It still needs leaders who will pressure the president and others to do the right thing, such as the role played by Martin Luther King in the Johnson administration. Well, if that's the case, then who are the real "leaders" of black America?

After all, despite the canonization of Martin Luther King today, we should remember that his popularity declined, and not all African-Americans believed he spoke for them. Some condemned him for speaking out against the Vietnam War and veering away from civil rights and into the realm of international human rights. And critics railed against his call for economic justice and a radical redistribution of wealth in America.

Where are the black leaders today? For example, seemingly ubiquitous leaders such as Rev. Sharpton always stood up for the families of slain police brutality victims, and for victims of gun violence such as Trayvon Martin. Across the nation, people have known that you always call Rev. Al in an emergency. And now, he has emerged as a national figure with a cable news program on MSNBC, and more access to the White House than any African-American leader.

Arnold Ahlert, former New York Post columnist, however, sees Sharpton in a different light. In the early days of the Trayvon Martin case, he scrutinized Sharpton's role in the protests.

"Al Sharpton remains one of the driving forces behind the effort to turn the Trayvon Martin case into an indictment of America itself. To earn his daily bread, Sharpton is well aware that he must continuously convince black Americans that they live in a hopelessly racist nation, not because it's true, but because any genuine progress made by blacks themselves is inimical to his own interests. Forgotten in the controversy surrounding the Martin case are the dark levels Sharpton has stooped to in order to ensure the survival of his public persona, which are worth recalling here.

"Sharpton's involvement in the Martin controversy hews to a familiar tune. Earlier this week, he held a protest with Rev. Jesse Jackson attended by thousands in Sanford, Florida, the town where Martin was shot. Sharpton has been working overtime instigating racial hatred, whipping up frenzied crowds with a false narrative. Presenting a petition demanding the immediate arrest of George Zimmerman, Martin's alleged shooter, Sharpton warned that if the board does not act swiftly, the town could become "the Birmingham of the 21st century, as a place of racial intolerance and double standards." He later asserted, "This is America on trial."

"By any reasonable standard, Sharpton's first brush with national prominence should have been his last. In 1987, Sharpton involved himself with a 15-year-old black girl named Tawana Brawley, who claimed that she had been abducted and raped in Dutchess County, New York. She had been missing for four days, and was found covered in dog feces with racial slurs written on her body. Ms. Brawley claimed that as many as six white men, one of whom carried a badge, had participated in the crime. Brawley refused to cooperate with prosecutors, which Sharpton characterized as "asking someone who watched someone killed in the gas chamber to sit down with Mr. Hitler."

"Absent a shred of evidence, Sharpton then went on to claim that a local prosecutor named Steven Pagones "had kidnapped, abused and raped" Brawley on "33 separate occasions." After Pagones was quickly cleared, Sharpton claimed a local police cult with ties to the Irish Republican

Army had perpetrated the crime. When a security guard for Sharpton and the rest of his legal team testified that Sharpton, et al., knew Brawley was lying, the case fell apart. In 1988, a grand jury concluded the entire case was a hoax.

"Pagones successfully sued Sharpton and his two accomplices in 1997, winning $345,000. Sharpton's share came to $65,000, all of which was paid off by a group of supporters, including lawyer Johnnie Cochran of O.J. Simpson fame. During testimony in the case, Sharpton claimed he "couldn't recall" any of the slanderous statements he made against Pagones. Sharpton remains unrepentant. Asked on a segment of "60 Minutes" why he never apologized for false accusations, Sharpton said, "I don't know that. I have thought about that a million times. I just don't believe they treated that case fair," he added.

"Fairness and Al Sharpton are mutually exclusive. 1991, after 7-year-old black boy Gavin Cato was run over and killed by a driver in a Hasidic Jewish rabbi's entourage in Brooklyn's Crown Heights neighborhood, Sharpton once again fanned the flames of racial animosity. In a eulogy given at Cato's funeral, Sharpton, in an anti-Semitic rant compared Crown Heights to segregationist South Africa. "The world will tell us he was killed by accident. Yes, it was a social accident...It's an accident to allow an apartheid ambulance service in the middle of Crown Heights...Talk about how Oppenheimer in South Africa sends diamonds straight to Tel Aviv and deals with the diamond merchants right here in Crown Heights. The issue is not anti-Semitism; the issue is apartheid...All we want to say is what Jesus said: If you offend one of these little ones, you got to pay for it. No compromise, no meetings, no kaffe klatsch, no skinnin' and grinnin'. Pay for your deeds."

"During three nights of black riots targeting Jewish homes and businesses, Jewish rabbinical student Yankel Rosenbaum was killed after being surrounded by a gang of youths and stabbed, while shouts of "kill the Jew" filled the air. Since Rosenbaum was killed the night before the eulogy, Sharpton bears no direct responsibility for his death. Yet there is no doubt about his determination to stoke violence. He took marchers along Eastern Parkway, leading the now-familiar chants, "Whose Streets? Our Streets," and "No Justice, No Peace."

"In 1992, Sharpton blew off an accusation by the Anti-Defamation League that he helped to incite anti-Semitism during the riots. "You don't even have a direct quote from me that anyone can call anti-Semitic," he contended, in yet another apparent memory lapse similar to the one he had during the Tawana Brawley hoax.

"This was not Sharpton's final attempt to immunize himself from accountability. When Fred Harari, the Jewish owner of Freddie's Fashion Mart, a clothing store located on 125th Street in Harlem, terminated a sublease agreement he had with a black tenant, Sikhulu Shange, who owned The Record Shack, Sharpton once again showed up to foment rage. It was an effort made irrespective of an inconvenient reality: Harari himself was a tenant who leased the space from the real landlord, the United House of Prayer for All People, a black Pentecostal church. The church used Harari to evict Shange instead of doing it themselves.

"Sharpton organized a picket line in front of the clothing store. On September 9, 1995, during a radio broadcast on station WWRL, Sharpton elucidated his reason for the picketing. "We will not stand by and allow them to move this brother, so that some white interloper can expand his business on 125th Street," he told listeners. "And we're asking the Buy Black Committee to go down there, and I'm gonna go down there, and do what is necessary to let them know that we are not turnin' 125th Street back over to outsiders as it was done in the early part of this century."

"The pickets continued into the fall, and one the participants, Roland J. Smith, aka Abubunde Mulocko, took Sharpton's message to heart. On December 8th, he entered Freddie's Fashion Mart with a loaded gun and ordered all black customers out of the store. He shot four people, set the store on fire and killed himself. Eight people were killed and, just as he did after Crown Heights, Sharpton absolved himself of any responsibility for the incident, claiming no one "connected me to the fire," and that his "only role was in fighting for justice in the same nonviolent manner I have my entire career."

Eric Hoffer wrote, "Every mass movement becomes a racket in the end." In many ways that describes the Civil Rights Movement as it finds its consequences today. Unlike the horrifically real abuses of the 1960s, today's movement depends largely on invented controversies and imaginary offenses.

The majestic leadership of Jesse Jackson settled down into a simple, concerted effort to extort contributions from major corporations. The New York Times called the Congressional Black Caucus a "fundraising juggernaut" as it soaked up the corporate dollar. The noble causes of the past had evaporated into contributions to finance people, not issues.

The cause defining the Civil Rights leaders of the 60s has turned into a career for today's pretenders. Karl Marx wrote that history does repeat itself, first as a tragedy and then as a farce. That is exactly what has happened in the long transition between Martin Luther King and Al Sharpton.

Fifty years ago the movement throughout the south told of sacrifice and bravery. It challenged racism in the streets and in the corridors of power. Today the ranting of the likes of Sharpton and Jackson instill racism as much as dispel it. The declarations of a fabricated oppression and abuse inspire young blacks to oppose their imaginary foe with force and rage. The violence spawned by the hatred shared by a generation of young blacks has been spelled out in blood across America.

In most social movements, leadership is found among intellectuals, professors, politicians, persons well known and respected for their insights and wisdom. That is not the case with the black community. At its highest level we find the same boiling hatred sent as messages to black youth.

We find a candid example of this point when studying the crime statistics involving forcible rape.

Of all the black on white violent crimes, forcible rape is the crime where race hatred is most evident. Unlike robbery, where there is an economic motive, brutal forcible rape is motivated by hatred and a desire to degrade and humiliate the victim. And when this rape is interracial and the perpetrators of of this crime are almost all from one race and the victims of another, then it is obvious that race hatred is a major factor in these crimes.

According to the "liberal" narrative on racism, systemic, pervasive, white racism is the racism that matters. And black racism is only grudgingly admitted to, if at all. Blacks can only be victims of racism according to this worldview, never the perpetrators of it.

So logically if this narrative is accurate, the interracial rape statistics should be overwhelmingly white on black.

Yet the opposite is true.

Unlike interracial robbery which has an economic motive, interracial rape, sexual homicide, and sexual assault, are crimes where race hatred is most clearly evident. This is not to say that interracial robbery cant have mixed motives, including racial hatred, but just that it is harder to isolate it.

Many sociologists say that rape by definition is a hate crime against women. And when that rape is interracial, brutal and murderous, then race hatred is obviously a factor as well.

The NCVS is an annual survey by the Department of Justice Statistics of almost 100,000 carefully selected American households designed to determine how much crime is not reported to the police. Crimes that are reported to the police are in the Uniform Crime Reports compiled annually by the FBI. The National Crime Victimization Survey of 2008 revealed 19,242 white victims of rape and sexual assault by blacks and zero black victims of white offenders.

As astonishing as the numbers may be, they were vast improvements over prior years such as 2007 when there were 32,443 white victims of rape and sexual assault by blacks and still zero Black victims of white offenders.

The 2005 report indicated that there had been 37,460 white victims of black offenders and zero black victims of white offenders.

Blacks seem to condone raping white women and some of their leaders have actually encouraged it. A racist revenge motive was openly admitted by Black Power Leader of the 1960s, Eldridge Cleaver, an admitted rapist of white women in his seminal book."Soul on Ice"

"Rape was an insurrectionary act. It delighted me that I was defying and trampling upon the white man's law, upon his system of values, and that I was defiling his women – and this point, I believe, was the most satisfying to me because I was very resentful over the historical fact of how the white man has used the black woman. I felt I was getting revenge.

Cleaver boasted of his rapes of blacks and whites and later in his writings bragged about how brutal they were.

"I started out practicing on black girls in the ghetto where dark and vicious deeds appear not as aberrations or deviations from the norm, but as part of the sufficiency of the evil of the day. When I considered myself smooth enough, I crossed the tracks and sought out white prey, I did this consciously, deliberately, willfully, methodically."

With this vicious crime so prevalent, where are the voices of the intellectual black leaders offering protest and guidance?

Black poet Amiri Baraka composed for his black readers, "Come up, black dada nihilismus. Rape the white girls. Rape their fathers. Cut the mothers' throats." Baraka held the honor of being the second poet laureate in the history of New Jersey. His poetry was so offensive and damaging to youth that the position was terminated by the Governor.

Multiple evidences indicate that a core body of black leaders and intellectuals not only do nothing to stem the tide of black violence, but willingly contribute to it.

Leonard Jeffries, Chairman of the African-American Studies Department of the City College of New York, issued statements appearing in the May, 1995 issue of Rutherford magazine:

Q: But the black man is no longer a slave.

A: The slave should be waking up, thinking of ways to slit the slave master's throat.

Q: What kind of world do you want to leave to your children?

A: A world in which there aren't any white people.

Dr. Kamau Kambon, former visiting professor of African Studies at NC State University, made the following remarks at "Black Media Forum on the Image of Black Americans in Mainstream Media." This was a program presented on October 14th at Howard University and broadcast by C-SPAN. Howard is termed a "historically black" university so Kambon was addressing black youth with this message.

"And then finally I want to say that we need one idea, and we're not thinking about a solution to the problem … And the one idea is, how we are going to exterminate white people because that in my estimation is the only conclusion I have come to. We have to exterminate white people off the face of the planet to solve this problem … [We need to] get very serious and not be diverted from coming up with a solution to the problem and the problem on the planet is white people."

Frances Cress Welsing, black psychiatrist, wrote in her *The Isis Papers: The Keys to the Colors*, "On both St. Vanlentine's Day and Mother's Day, the white male gives gifts of chocolate candy with nuts … If his sweetheart ingests 'chocolate with nuts,' the white male can fantasize that he is genetically equal to the Black male."

A noted white psychiatrist responded by stating that by Welsing's reasoning, a black woman getting married in a white gown is subconsciously wishing the groom was white.

Chancellor Williams (Afrocentrist and author of The Destruction of Black Civilization) — "The necessary re-education of Blacks and a possible solution of the racial crisis can begin … only when Blacks fully realize this central fact to their lives: the white man is their Bitter Enemy."

John Street, black ex-mayor of Philadelphia, made local politics racist by shouting, "Let me tell you: The brothers and sisters are running this city. Oh yes. The brothers and sisters are running this city. Running it! Don't let nobody fool you; we are in charge of the City of Brotherly Love. We are in charge! We are in charge!"

It is easily forgotten that South Carolina was one of the states where blacks demanded an end to discrimination but no one taught that to black state senator Kay Patterson who sent invitations to black politicians with the notation,

"Now please don't bring any of your 'White-Friends,' this is a 'Colored' meeting."

The late jazz musician Miles Davis stated, "If somebody told me I had only one hour to live, I'd spend it choking a white man. I'd do it nice and slow."

Nathan McCall, black journalist for the Washington Post wrote in his autobiography *Makes Me Wanna Holler,* "The fellas and I were hanging out on our corner one afternoon when the strangest thing happened. A white boy ... came pedaling a bicycle casually through the neighborhood. ... Somebody spotted him and pointed him out to the rest of us. 'Look! What's that motherfucka doin' ridin' through here?! Is he crraaaazy?!' ... We caught him on Cavalier Boulevard and knocked him off the bike. ...

Ignoring the passing cars, we stomped him and kicked him. My stick partners kicked him in the head and face and watched the blood gush from his mouth. I kicked him in the stomach and nuts, where I knew it would hurt. Every time I drove my foot into his balls, I felt better ... one dude kept stomping, like he'd gone berserk ... When he finished, he reached down and picked up the white dude's bike, lifted it as high as he could above his head, and slammed it down on him hard. ... We walked away, laughing, boasting, competing for bragging rights about who'd done the most damage."

Gus Savage, former U.S. Representative from Chicago told a white member of the press, "I don't talk to you white motherfuckers ... You bitch motherfuckers in the white press ... Fuck you, you motherfucking asshole ... white devils."

Khalid Abdul Muhammed, former assistant to Louis Farrakhan, current leader of the New Black Panther Party, evidently didn't believe that movies should be made dealing with reality when he said, 'Hollywood is owned by these so-called Jews. Look at the movies they make about us, Black people killing Black people. Let's make some revolutionary movies where we kill white people in the movie. Kill 'em so hard you have to cover up your popcorn from the blood spraying out of the screen." This was, of course, a speech at San Francisco State University, to young students.

Khalid Abdul Muhammed spoke to young people at Kean College in Union, New Jersey about what should be done if white people do not leave South Africa to the blacks. "We kill the women. We kill the babies. We kill the blind. We kill the cripples. We kill them all ... When you get through killing them all, go to the goddamn graveyard and kill them a-goddamn-gain because they didn't die hard enough."

Supreme Court Justice Thurgood Marshall (in a conversation with Justice William Douglas about racial preferences) "You guys have been practicing discrimination for years. Now it is our turn."

Sister Souljah (rap artist and black activist) "If black people kill black people every day, why not have a week and kill white people."

Amiri Baraka, black poet and writer, spewed more of his venom of hate to black youth with, "All the stores will open up if you will say the magic words. The magic words are: Up against the wall motherfucker this is a stick up!"

When a plane crashed in 1962, Malcolm X stated, "The death of over 120 white people is a very beautiful thing."

When protests were made against black comments targeting whites as targets of hate and violence, Mary Frances Berry, head of U.S. Commission on Civil Rights, made the astonishing statement, "Civil rights laws were not passed to protect the rights of white men and do not apply to them."

Who would dare suggest that the inflammatory statements from noted black people would not influence the minds of the young? How can the same, reportedly intelligent leaders ignore the results? Each one is an accomplice to every black crime and none has the ability to recognize it.

Blacks like to make claims like "you never see a black serial killer!" but it's simply another of the fallacies. One can only imagine what distinction might be found if it were true that no black serial killers existed but the claim is consistently made, "You never see a black serial killer!"

It is a common myth that blacks are under-represented in the serial killer population. For instance, if you do an Yahoo image search for serial killers, hundreds of photos pop up and almost all of them are white.

But blacks are actually overrepresented in the population with some studies showing that adult black males who make up less than 5 percent of the population comprise up to 21 percent of the serial killers .

With the beginning of the 1970s, the number of serial Killer cases exploded and much of the reason was blacks beginning a long history of killing sprees.

In a sample of 413 serial killers operating in the United States from 1945 to mid-2004, it was found that 90 were African American. Relative to the African American proportion of the population across that time period, African Americans were overrepresented in the ranks of serial killers by a factor of about 2 to 1. Data from 2000 to 2010 prove that black serial killers actually outnumbered white serial killers.

Matthew Emmannuel Mason killed six white victims. Cleophus Prince (the Clairemont Killer) had six white victims. Anthony and Nathaniel Cook claimed nine white victims in their eight-year killing spree.

The "Westside Rapist" who stalked, raped and murdered at least 30 elderly women was black John Floyd Thomas, Jr. Detectives describe John Floyd Thomas Jr as one of the region's most prolific serial killers, saying that he remains a suspect in at least 10 to 15 additional slayings.

An obvious metric of black racial hatred is when black serial killers chose to kill almost exclusively white victims.

Take the case of black interracial serial killer, Coral Eugene Watts, black, who stalked and murdered almost 100 young white women in a 20 year rampage.

Who can forget that the Washington D.C. "Beltway Snipers," John Allen Muhammad, 45, and his accomplice, Lee Boyd Malvo, 21, were black and guilty of slaying seven people?

Kendall Francois, black, is a serial killer from Poughkeepsie, New York, convicted of killing eight women, from 1996 to 1998.[1] He is currently serving life in prison for his crimes.

Reginald and Kevin Haley, black, participated in an estimated 500 burglaries, 60 rapes, and eight murders over a five-year period ending with their arrest in 1984.

It is difficult to find a crime category where black youth do not represent the most prolific offenders. Statistics and studies seemingly have no impact upon the conscience of blacks given roles of leadership and responsibility. Instead of inspiring the youth to achieve and pursue cures for the social ills of their community, they fill them with messages of hate and criminal terror.

The bottom line is that nothing is being done. The epidemic of black crime spreads and infects while society gets stuck on white-on-black deaths hawked by black leaders into an international frenzy. All the while they ignore that in the 513 days between Trayvon dying, and he Zimmerman verdict, more than 9,000 African-Americans were murdered by other African-Americans. More blacks were being killed in Chicago than in the killing fields of Afghanistan. Six deaths have been recorded due to the senseless black youth knockout game.

The apathy of black leaders not only suggest that crimes are unimportant to their agenda but that the young offenders are unimportant as well. Their anti-white doctrine has millions of young black converts desensitized to violence and death involving white victims.

Grace Watkins, black 18-year-old New Yorker, commented on two policemen killed in a shootout at the Stapleton Houses project where she lives: "I think a lot of people out here weren't worried about [the killings] because they thought they were white cops. But when they heard the cops were black, they're attitude changed totally and they started expressing concern for the police officers' families."

With an anemic understanding of slavery, modern blacks continue to seek vengeance for its existence in the colonial period of America into the 19th century. Whites of today are seen as equally guilty of slavery as the whites of the 1700s who actually owned slaves. It would be the same logic if whites of today blamed blacks for the savagery and cannibalism of the black Mau Maus of Africa in the 1950s. Gray Leakey, great-uncle of the white Kenyan politician and conservationist Richard Leakey and a blood-brother of the Kikuyu tribe from which the movement was drawn, was buried alive after some of his extremities had been eaten by his Mau Mau captors.

Throughout the history of Africa, women were the most common slaves used for domestic and field work. The number of slave women a man held often symbolized his personal wealth. Slaves were gained as prisoners taken in battle or purchased in slave markets.

Some African societies held laws maintaining that the children of slaves could not be sold and that freedom could be obtained after three or four generations of slavery.

It was not surprising then when Europeans negotiated for African slaves and found them through African sellers. Whites often like to make the claim, "Blacks sold their own people into slavery!" It's true but not as historically offensive as one might think. Slavery had been around a long time in Africa. The early dynasties of Egypt acquired slaves from Africa around the same time that the Jews were cast into slavery. In the late 5th century BC, Romans followed the Greeks in attacking North Africa in search of black slaves. Arab Muslims later followed the practice.

Arabs had a thriving slave trade business for centuries and it was an accepted social practice to own one or two. After all, the Qurán and Islamic law justified slavery. The Arabs had extensive black slave trafficking into Turkey, Persia and India.

It is estimated that more than ten million black men, women and children were captured and sold into slavery by those in the Saharan slave trade that lasted more than a thousand years.

By the 15th century, Portuguese traders appeared on the African coast and were soon followed by the British and the French. Blacks like to claim that their enslaved forefathers founded America because whites were too lazy to do it for themselves. This is another fantasy. The government of Britain recognized the vast agricultural potential of the New World and that there were not enough colonists to provide all the products that could be gained. It was determined that slaves could speed the process along significantly.

It wasn't only independent black slave traders that provided the workers for the New World. Government of black nations started to enter the slave business and gained even more by enslaving people as punishment for crimes and religious offenses.

Modern blacks hold to the belief that they were unique in their historic posture as slaves and that is yet another fallacy. History books call them "indentured servants" but that is totally misrepresentative of historic fact. Slaves from Ireland also came on slave ships. Hundreds of thousands of men, women and children came to be the property of slave owners. Rebellious Irish slaves were hung by their hands and their hands and feet would be set on fire as punishment. Some were burned alive and their heads were placed on spikes in the marketplace to warn other slaves of the price of disobedience.

The Irish slave trade began when King James II sold more than thirty thousand Irish prisoners into slavery. They were to be taken on slave ships to the New World and sold into slavery to the colonists. Ireland was a source of slaves greater than Africa for a time and the majority of slaves in the New World were Irish, not black.

In the eleven years between 1641 and 1652, more than 300,000 Irish were sold into slavery and the population of Ireland was decreased to less than half of what it was before slavery began. Irish slave men were not permitted to take their wives and children with them to the New World and that created many helpless women and babies left to hunger and poverty. The king's answer was to sell them into slavery as well.

In the 1650s, more than 100,000 children from Ireland were forcibly taken from their parents and sold into slavery in the West Indies and the American colonies. 30,000 Irish men and women were put in the slave markets.

Young black youths lament the enslavement of their forefathers while ignoring, or never knowing, of the hundreds of thousands of white slaves worked to death long before the first black slave arrived to the New World. Like the blacks to come later, their children were born into slavery, too. A child born to a white slave was considered to also be a slave for life. The same vile treatment later given to the black was suffered by white Irishmen long before. Wives were sold on the block and separated from their husbands who were sold to other masters. Their children were sold to yet other owners and forever lost to their parents. During the time of this massive wave of white slavery, there were free blacks walking the streets of the colonial cities.

Historian Michael J. Hoffman II states, "I challenge any researcher to study 17th century colonial America, sifting the documents, the jargon and the statutes on both sides of the Atlantic and one will discover that White slavery was a far more extensive operation than Black enslavement."

Hoffman presents the account, "In 1855, Frederic Law Olmsted, the landscape architect who designed New York's Central Park, was in Alabama on a pleasure trip and saw bales of cotton being thrown from a considerable height into a cargo ship's hold. The men tossing the bales somewhat recklessly into the hold were Negroes, the men in the hold were Irish.

"Olmsted inquired about this to a ship worker. "Oh," said the worker, "the niggers are worth too much to be risked here; if the Paddies are knocked overboard or get their backs broke, nobody loses anything."

John Van Der Zee's book, *Bound Over*, tells of the wholesale kidnapping of young boys to be sold into slavery. "Press gangs in the hire of local merchants roamed the streets, seizing 'by force such boys as seemed proper subjects for the slave trade.' Children were driven in flocks through the town and confined for shipment in barns...So flagrant was the practice that people in the countryside about Aberdeen avoided bringing children into the city for fear they might be stolen; and so widespread was the collusion of merchants, shippers, suppliers and even magistrates that the man who exposed it was forced to recant and run out of town."

Slave ships bringing Irish slaves to the Americas used the same techniques as later with blacks. All the men slaves were kept below deck in chains. The journey would take from nine to twelve weeks and the death rate was horrendous. Available statistics indicate the death rate of white slaves was higher than that of the blacks.

In his writings, Foster R. Dulles states that ". . . often as many as 300 passengers on little vessels of not more than 200 tons burden--overcrowded, unsanitary...The mortality rate was sometimes as high as 50% and young children seldom survived the horrors of a voyage which might last anywhere from seven to twelve weeks."

Today's young blacks, touting past slavery as a cause for modern delinquency, never obtain sufficient education to know that eighty percent of all the white slaves sold to the sugar plantations of the West Indies did not survive the first year.

Hoffman contends that, "The chronicle of White slavery in America comprises the dustiest shelf in the darkest corner of suppressed American history. Should the truth about that epoch ever emerge into the public consciousness of Americans, the whole basis for the swindle of "Affirmative action," "minority set-asides" and proposed "Reparations to African-Americans" will be swept away. The fact is, the white working people of this country owe no one. They are themselves the descendants, as Congressman Wilmot so aptly said, of "the sons of toil."

But the slavery card is played by self-serving black leaders and subservient whites afraid to speak the truth. Susan Sontag says she is ashamed of being white without considering that after centuries of international slavery, if white men owned slaves, it was white men who also freed them. If there were generations of suffering, it was white men who established by law, that it would never happen again.

BLACK

Those who will not reason are bigots,
those who cannot, are fools,
and those who dare not, are slaves.
George Gordon Byron

THE GREATER QUESTION

"The negative effects of slavery have been theoretically linked to contemporary problems faced by African Americans, such as family instability, low achievement motivation, and high rates of juvenile delinquency and youth violence," says Dr. William E. Cross, Jr., one of America's leading theorists on black identity development. Other researchers and experts agree with him.

There remains, however, a greater question demanding to be addressed.

Scotland Yard has openly accused the black community of England for the majority of violent crime as reported by the London Daily Mail of June 27, 2010.

"Among those proceeded against for street crimes, including muggings, assault with intent to rob and snatching property, 54 per cent were black males," says the article.

"On sex offences, black men made up 32 per cent of all male suspects, with 49 per cent of those apprehended by police being white men.

"The statistics also suggest that police hold black women accountable for a disproportionate amount of violent crime. On knife crime, 45 per cent of suspected female perpetrators were black. Among those women and girls police took action against for gun crime, 58 per cent were black and in robberies that figure was 52 per cent.

"The police statistics relate to those prosecuted - whether convicted or acquitted. . . ."

Only 3% of England's population is negro and yet Scotland Yard is crediting the majority of crime to the black segment of society.

When the Dec. 1, 2011 issue of Business Insider listed the world's 20 most homicidal nations, eleven of them had black populations. Of the world's population, Fifty-five percent are Orientals and fifteen percent are black and yet blacks murdered 24,500 more people in 2013 than all Orientals.

Of the 22 island nations of the Caribbean, the majority of the black population is found on Haiti, Dominican Republic, Jamaica and Cuba that together create a murder rate second only to Africa.

One cannot avoid the question, if the experts are correct and slavery is a contributing factor to delinquency, why do we find the same tendency to black violence across the world? The blacks of England did not experience the American slavery experience and yet are producing the highest crime level of any segment of society.

Australia's Lake Elliott News reports: The brutal bashing of a young (White) man at Sunshine train station in Melbourne (Australia) has highlighted the problems of crime associated with the immigration of large numbers of black Africans into Australia.

"Professor Andrew Frasier warned us all in 2005 about these dangers, when he said: "Experience, practically everywhere in the world, tells us that an expanding black population is a sure-fire recipe for increases in crime, violence and a wide range of other social problems." Fraser was persecuted by the so-called "Human Rights" industry for telling the truth.

Newspaper reports in Australia have confirmed the higher crime rates of Black Africans. For instance, the Herald Sun revealed that whilst the general rate of alleged crimes was 1 in 85... the rate for Somalians was 1 in 23.

Political multiculturalists may offer all sorts of excuses as to why the Black African crime rate is so much higher in Australia, blaming poverty, war trauma, etc., but the fact remains that their crime rate is indeed higher.

French citizens are increasingly bitter that their government permitted extensive black immigration. The popular wave of resentment has led to the formation of an anti-immigrant political party, the Front National. France now suffers areas that have been called "non-white gangland areas, marked by extreme social deprivation and crime." One report states, "In October 2005, a wave of non-White rioting hit France, perpetrated by North African gangs across the country. Thousands of cars were burned, and at least one person was killed in the unrest. However, the 2005 riots were not an isolated incident, but in fact part of pattern that has grown along with the increasing non-white population. Colombes, a suburb of 85,000 north-west of Paris was crippled by a crime wave involving black drug dealers.

In Holland, Richard Nieuwenhuizen was doing what he loved: watching his son play football and helping out his local club by running the touchline as a volunteer linesman. The 41-year-old father's passion for football cost him his life.

Dutch prosecutors announced they were charging three players, two 15-year-olds and a 16-year-old, with manslaughter, assault and public violence for alleged involvement in a vicious attack on Nieuwenhuizen after a youth match between two local clubs.

A group of Nieuw Sloten players surrounded Nieuwenhuizen and kicked and punched him after the match against his son's team on Sunday. Nieuwenhuizen went home to lie down, and returned later to watch another game, where he collapsed and was rushed to hospital. He died the next day.

All the players on both teams were white except the three that attacked Nieuwenhuizen who were black Moroccans.

Apart from the black reasoning that slavery somehow contributes to modern delinquency, we also hear the excuse that black crime is driven by poverty. But Michael Vick had made $150 million dollars at the time he decided to try his hand at illegal dog fighting. Bam Morris, the Kansas City Chief running back, earned $1.3 million the year he decided to distribute drugs. Michael Irvin had earned millions as a Dallas Cowboy when he was arrested with cocaine in his possession. More Dallas Cowboys, Troy Hambrick, was making mega bucks when he sold crack to an undercover officer and Thomas "Hollywood" Henderson was earning millions when he was convicted of sexual assault.

Willie Aikins was earning $365,000 a year which was big time cash in the 1980s when he decided to be a drug dealer. Allen Iverson was making millions when he accumulated five arrests for a variety of charges. Mike

Tyson earned $300 million and still spent time in prison and has had several brushes with the law since.

The list could be a book in itself and raises the question whether or not the poverty claim is valid. By all evidences, blacks resort to crime and violence with or without money. Blacks take great pride in noting that they have become the majority in professional sports. Perhaps that would explain why the 1,696 players in the NFL have accumulated an astounding 664 arrests. Even O.J. got a whopping get-out-of-jail-free card but still couldn't stay out of prison.

Bertil Fox, internationally known black champion bodybuilder, set aside his career to murder his ex-fiancée. Clifford "The Black Rhino" Etienne enjoyed a successful boxing career in which he had 29 wins in 35 fights. Interestingly enough, he began boxing while serving a prison sentence for armed robbery. After earning numerous awards for his post-prison boxing career, Etienne found himself back behind bars in 2006 on charges of armed robbery, kidnapping and the attempted murder of a police officer during a crazy cocaine-fueled bender that involved robbing a business, carjacking and kidnapping a family and trying to shoot two cops. He was swiftly sent back to prison for 150 years without the chance of parole.

Darryl Henley, former black member of the Los Angeles Rams was convicted of drug trafficking and sentenced to 20 years in prison. He promptly hired a hit man to kill the judge and a witness only to be convicted of that crime and getting another 21 years added to his sentence.

Professional black soccer player Kevin Grant is serving life for murder. Jamaican cricket player, Leslie Hylton, was hanged in 1955 for murdering his wife.

Rae Carruth achieved fame with the Carolina Panthers when by reports, "In 1999, Carruth was driving in Charlotte, North Carolina, when he stopped his car to allow friend Van Brett Watkins to shoot a woman in the adjacent car four times. That woman was a carrying Carruth's child at the time. The child was saved by doctors but the woman died. After a brief period during which Carruth was a fugitive, he was convicted of conspiracy to commit first-degree murder, shooting into an occupied vehicle and using an instrument to destroy an unborn child. Carruth was sentenced to 18 years and 11 months in prison."

The historic excuses for black crime do not seem to be supported by statistical evidences. If that is the case, however, the somber alternative is that blacks have a physical or emotional impetus to be criminals.

Certainly there are various environmental issues. The predominance of single parent homes and the breakdown of the family structure could contribute to youth crime. Households headed by women, numerous illegitimate births and revolving door relationships also are factors. Anthropologist Patricia Draper of Pennsylvania State University studied black domestic relationships in the U.S., Caribbean and Africa and found that the slavery legacy excuse is not valid since blacks having a heritage of slavery or not produce the same insecurities in their homes and levels of delinquency.

She suggests that biological variables such as the sex hormone testosterone are implicated in the tendency toward multiple relationships as well as the tendency to commit crime. One study, published in the 1993 issue of Criminology by Alan Booth and D. Wayne Osgood, showed clear evidence of a testosterone-crime link based on an analysis of 4,462 U.S. military personnel. Other studies have linked testosterone to an aggressive and impulsive personality, to a lack of empathy, and to sexual behavior. Testosterone levels explain why young men are disproportionately represented in crime statistics relative to young women, and why younger people are more trouble-prone than older people. Testosterone reliably differentiates the sexes and is known to decline with age

Ethnic differences exist in average level of testosterone. Studies show 3 to 19 percent more testosterone in black college students and military veterans than in their white counterparts. Studies among the Japanese show a correspondingly lower amount of testosterone than among white Americans. Medical research has focused on cancer of the prostate, one determinant of which is testosterone. Black men have higher rates of prostate cancer than do white men who in turn have higher rates than do Oriental men.

Studies have also demonstrated that racial differences may well cause variants in sexual behavior. The results indicate that blacks are sexually active at an earlier age, have more sexual partners and are more likely to view the act as purely physical rather than relating it to any emotion.

About 50% of testosterone and its metabolites are heritable. Crime studies have given sound evidence that criminal tendencies can also be inherited. Research into this premise ranks among the most interesting in decades. Adoption agencies in the United States, Denmark and Sweden kept records that were later assessed to reveal that children adopted in infancy had a higher risk of criminal conviction if their biological parents had been convicted. The rate remained higher even in cases where the adopted parent was convicted. The research involved a total of 14,427 adoptions over a period of 33 years.

Racial differences also exist in average IQ-test scores and again the pattern extends well beyond the United States. The global literature on IQ was reviewed by Richard Lynn in the 1991 issue of Mankind Quarterly. Caucasoids of North America, Europe, and Australasia generally obtained mean IQs of around 100. Mongoloids from both North America and the Pacific Rim obtained slightly higher means, in the range of 101 to 111. Africans from south of the Sahara, African-Americans, and African-Caribbeans (including those living in Britain) obtained mean IQs ranging from 70 to 90.

Racial differences exist at a more profound level than is normally considered. Why do Europeans average so consistently between Africans and Asians in crime, family system, sexual behavior, testosterone level, intelligence, and brain size? It is almost certain that genetics and evolution have a role to play. Transracial adoption studies indicate genetic influence. Studies of Korean and Vietnamese children adopted into white American and white Belgian homes showed that, although as babies many had been hospitalized for malnutrition, they grew to excel in academic ability with IQs ten points higher than their adoptive national norms. By contrast, Sandra Scarr and her colleagues at Minnesota found that at age 17, black and mixed-race children adopted into white middle-class families performed at a lower level than the white siblings with whom they were raised. Adopted white children had an average IQ of 106, an average aptitude based on national norms at the 59th percentile, and a class rank at the 54th percentile; mixed-race children had an average IQ of 99, an aptitude at the 53rd percentile, and a class rank at the 40th percentile; and black children had an average IQ of 89, an aptitude at the 42nd percentile, and a class rank at the 36th percentile.

Physical, emotional and mental factors may well explain the black tendency toward criminal behavior but if true, it cannot explain why the majority of black society is hard-working, honest and responsible.

Harold Mangle of the National Institute of Human Behavior maintains that, "If a black kid goes to school, learns and becomes educated, he has no excuse for being a street wise criminal. If he drops out of school, however, and has a low level of knowledge, he can justify his criminality by his lack of education and other imaginary disadvantages.

"If he becomes educated and is later employed with a career, he has no reason to live in the projects or be influenced by the poverty surrounding him. But if he insists there are no jobs, he can blame his unemployment on social conditions.

"The entire existence of black youth is the process of inventing reasons to be unproductive and allegedly victimized."

There is no reason to suspect that Mangle is wrong. A child of any race is entitled to a free education. The National School Lunch Program provides free breakfast and midday meal to children in need. Most school districts provide transportation to and from school. What is left is the personal desire to learn, be responsible for academic work and seek opportunities for a higher education. To claim that the lack of education ranks with any form of disadvantage is nothing less than a lie.

The same pattern of using imaginary social ills to justify criminality is not unique to America. Blacks in South Africa are adept at doing the same.

"Rape is one of the most under-reported crimes in South Africa," noted Shukumisa, an NGO coalition. It points to research, conducted in Gauteng in 2010, that found one in four of women questioned in the study had been raped in the course of their lifetimes, while almost one in 12 had been raped in 2009. But only one in 13 women raped by a non-partner reported the incident to the police, while one in 25 of the women raped by their partner reported this to the police.

Lizette Lancaster, manager of the ISS crime and justice information hub, says there are many complex reasons South Africa has such high sexual offence rates. The armed struggle against apartheid and the violent backlash and suppression that followed have led to a normalization of violence in South African society, she said. "Kids grew up seeing violence on their streets," she added.

There always remains, however, the unmentionable. We find it in a November 1, 2001 article from London's *The Telegraph*.

"The alleged rape of a nine-month-old baby girl by six men in a remote part of rural South Africa last week has focused the nation on an 80 per cent rise in child sexual abuse over a year, much of it connected with the country's Aids pandemic.

"More than 67,000 cases of rape and sexual assaults against children were reported last year, compared with 37,500 in 1998. Child welfare groups believe that the number of unreported incidents could be up to 10 times that number.

"Some of the victims were as young as six-months-old, a number of whom died from their injuries, while others contracted HIV. The largest increase in attacks has been against children under seven.

"Although rises in poverty, violent crime and unemployment are said to have contributed to the escalation in child abuse, the most significant and worrying factor is the widespread myth sweeping the country that having sex with children provides a cure for Aids.

"Cati Vawda, the director of the Children's Rights Centre in Durban, said: 'There is a belief across South Africa that a virgin will cure a man of HIV or Aids. We have no idea where this idea has come from, but it has been around for a few years and has certainly taken hold.'

"Kelly Hatfield, of People Opposed to Women Abused , added: 'South Africa has reached a new low. This rumour certainly has become a common belief.'"

South Africa has the highest number of HIV-positive citizens in the world. According to official figures, one in nine South Africans are infected with the virus, although many health workers believe the rate of infection to be closer to one in eight. Schools often harbor the worst sex offenders. The deputy headmaster of South African school was accused of raping schoolgirls over a 10-year period, resulting in 20 of them becoming pregnant.

185 child abuse cases are reported to the police each day but represent only a fraction of the true number committed, according to child welfare groups. Of these, just five per cent result in a successful conviction.

Most child rape cases are not reported because child abusers are often relatives of their victims; even their fathers and providers. For women, making a complaint is a hard choice because they end up losing their husbands, the breadwinners and the roof over their heads.

Even though the monumental ignorance fostering such superstitions loom in a nation where ten percent of the people have never seen a day in school, young people among American blacks prefer to remain uneducated. For many, dealing drugs on the corner represents gainful employment. Even participating in this act of criminal behavior, however, becomes a racial issue when blacks complain of being profiled or targeted by police. The complaints became so frequent that the Human Rights Watch had to publish the notice:

"Although whites are relatively untouched by anti-drug efforts compared to blacks, supporters of the drug war may not see a problem of race discrimination because they do not believe the purpose of drug law enforcement is to harm blacks – if anything, drug law enforcement is seen as protecting minority communities from addiction, harassment, and violence."

The underlying message of the qualifying comment, however, is that blacks deal drugs with greater frequency than those of other races. The official report titled, *Offense Distribution of Inmates in State Prisons in the US 2011, by Race/Ethnicity and Gender,* ends with the summary statement, " . . . more black inmates were sentenced for drug offenses than inmates of other races or Hispanic origin." Under the section *People of Color in State Prison for Drug Offenses,* "The number of people in state prisons for drug offenses has increased 550 percent over the last 20 years."

The 2012 census reported 44,456,009 blacks living in the United States that accounted for a total of 2,640,067 arrests. As 14.2 percent of the national population, the reasonable share of the 9,390,473 total arrests for 2012 should have been 1,333,447 or 14.2 percent instead of the 29% of all arrest that were actually recorded. Whites represented 64% of the nation's population and roughly 69% of the year's arrests, a percentage far more representative and starkly different from the doubling of the black statistics.

Whatever reasons black youth invents for their plight, their criminal conduct is supported by black leaders who are little more than cheerleaders for crime. It is also the active cultivation of hostility and hatred which is purposely cultivated within black communities by black-oriented newspapers, radio, community organizers, religious clerics from their pulpits, black "leaders", academics, politicians, and mainstream media. The hatred and hostility are carefully cultivated into a wild resentment which often has no other outlet besides violence.

Still thumping the slavery drum to teach black youth the adversities of their lives that are, as always, the white man's fault, Al Sharpton issues comments like:

"It is true that Mr. Lincoln signed the Emancipation Proclamation, after which thee was a commitment to give 40 acres and a mule. That's where the argument, to this day, of reparations starts. We never got the 40 acres. We went all the way to Herbert Hoover, and we never got the 40 acres. We didn't get the mule. So we decided we'd ride this donkey as far as it would take us."

If Sharpton does little else, he needs to brush up on his history. First of all, the commitment was not 40 acres of land, rather, the order stated "a plot of not more than (40) acres" which means it could have been significantly less. The original proposal did not include a mule and officially never did. It was merely a suggestion made by General Sherman that a mule could also be given.

Moreover, it would not be 40 acres wherever an ex-slave wanted it. The order stated clearly, "a strip of coastline stretching from Charleston, South Carolina, to the St. John's River in Florida, including Georgia's Sea Islands and the mainland thirty miles in from the coast."

Upon the death of Abraham Lincoln, the entire program was vetoed by President Andrew Johnson and the Congress chose not to override the veto. To this day, 150 years later, those like Sharpton are complaining about it and hawking the idea of reparation.

It is reminiscent of the bonus promised to World War I veterans wherein veterans up to the rank of major with a minimum of 60 days of military service would receive a bonus up to $625 dollars. The sudden appearance of the great depression, however, made payment impossible and in spite of more than 100,000 veterans marching on the capitol and demanding payment.

The bonus was never paid but who has heard of any continuing demands or tear shedding over this failure of the government that actually amounted to more money in 1920 than did the promised land to blacks in 1866.

Sharpton's mastery of human history was also shown in his statement:

"White folks was in the caves while we [blacks] was building empires ... We built pyramids before Donald Trump ever knew what architecture was ... we taught philosophy and astrology and mathematics before Socrates and them Greek homos ever got around to it."

No one thought it would serve a good purpose to tell Al that there is absolutely no evidence to support the idea that pyramid-building Egyptians were black. The attempt has been made by generations of blacks to prove this point but the question largely came to a climax with the recreation of the face belonging to Tutankhamun that failed to sufficiently match negroid features and it brought a wave of protests from blacks wanting the restoration to be evidence to their claims. At last, to resolve the point, Secretary General of the Egyptian Supreme Council of Antiquities, Dr. Zahi Hawass stated that "Tutankhamun was not black."

Likewise, Sharpton found no problem in using the "homo" word that offended countless gays but protested loudly when Don Imus spoke of "nappy headed hos." To echo the black use of "ho" to insult women was offensive to Sharpton but "homo," in his opinion, should not offend anyone.

In one poll of black citizens, Al Sharpton was chosen as the most preferred leader of the black community. As a leader, we must assume that would mean you would want him to be the one to provide guidance and leadership to your children.

In 1991, however, a seven-year-old black child was accidentally killed by a car driven by a Hasidic Jew. As tragic as it was, it should have been considered an accident and concluded in the traditional, legal ways. But entered Al Sharpton with his typical rants to enrage his audiences. For three days after there were anti-Jew riots challenging anything seen in Nazi Germany. Signs appeared claiming that Hitler had not done the job. Two innocent men were killed only because black rioters believed they were Jews.

Sharpton denied any responsibility, saying that he had not mentioned anything about violence.

Al uses the slavery card at any opportunity and serves only to give young blacks the sense of entitlement to their delinquency. Not even the rather neutral issue of raising the minimum wage could escape his slavery-themed rhetoric as he shouted:

". . . . blacks suffer disproportionately from having to do work and not get the kind of wages that we need. This is a central concern in our community. It's not just having a job; but having wages that are guaranteed to provide for our families. We had full employment in the black community during slavery. We just didn't have wages. So we don't want just a job, we want a job that pays, and pays so that we can take care of our families."

Dr. Carol Swain, black professor of law and political science at Vanderbilt University, agrees that black leaders like Sharpton do little to truly serve their people. She uses the Trayvon Martin case to emphasize her point, stating that the majority of the people wanted an investigation of the case but when the so-called black leaders came on the scene, "it quickly became a racial issue fueling racial divide in America," Swain said.

An expert on race relations and author of *Be the People: A Call to Reclaim America's Faith and Promise,* Swain maintains that black leaders "don't put forth ideas and solutions that advance the cause of black people," Swain said. Rather, they "prefer to heat up the situation."

In one interview she claimed that black leaders benefit from characterizing events as motivated by racism because it can be used for voter mobilization. She noted that there were voter registration drives at many of the Martin protest rallies.

"There are so many cases of heinous behavior in our black communities," Swain said and she remains an open critic of Obama's reference to the Martin case while so many others with white victims of black violence were ignored.

"Black people have been encouraged to hate whites and to discriminate against them from the so-called civil rights leaders," said author and syndicated talk show host Jesse Lee Peterson:"And that is evil. The evil will get worse from generation to generation if you don't deal with it."

Taleeb Starkes is a social worker, and author of the book called *The Un-Civil War.* Starks strongly objects to the classroom messages of victimization of blacks.

"These schools are reinforcing the long-existing, deep-rooted, victimization gospel that's religiously practiced in the African-American community," said Starkes. "Moreover, denunciation of this victimization gospel by any African-American is sacrilegious and leads to the questioning of 'blackness.' Even scarier is the fact that this ideology is spawning urban terrorists whose actions are always justified by another tenet of the victimization gospel called P.T.S.D (Post Traumatic Slavery Disorder)."

Starkes continued, "Combined with the race peddlers and the mainstream media's intentional portrayal of African-Americans as permanent victims incapable of hate-crimes, this self-defeating ideology has become a societal toxin. Consequently, any Black-on-White crime, regardless of viciousness, is essentially interpreted as Black 'payback' instead of Black crime."

Reasonable approaches like Swain's and Starkes' are far too few and far between. Instead, modern black youth have the likes of Louis Farrakhan who ended a Nation of Islam conference with his plan for blacks to separate from white America and for all of them to move to Detroit and establish their own justice system.

"We want equal justice under the law. Our people can't take much more. We have to have our own courts. You failed us," he charged.

We dare ask the black youth of America to find new, productive lives when a black leader tries to lead them to sedition? On one occasion he asked the crowd if the United States had treated them fairly. The response came in a loud, "No!" It was then Farrakhan told the government, "So, if we retaliate, you can bring out your soldiers. We got some, too!"

It would be ridiculously naïve, like Sharpton, to believe that such rhetoric does not have consequences. In Atlanta, Georgia, three young girls were shot down by a black man. The motive for the attack? They were white.

Nkosi Thandiwe was sentenced to life in prison plus 65 years for shooting the girls. One died and one is paralyzed.

When the court sought a motive for the attack, Thandiwe testified that he bought a pistol "to enforce beliefs he'd developed about white people during his later years as an anthropology major at the University of West Georgia."

"I was trying to prove a point that Europeans had colonized the world, and as a result of that, we see a lot of evil today," he said. "In terms of slavery and race, it was something that needed to be answered for. I saw it as something that the black community hasn't recovered from so my initial way to handle that was to spread information to help combat some of the ignorance that was in the black community about our history," said Thandiwe.

"Correct me if I'm wrong, but you were trying to spread the message of making white people the enemy," asked Assistant District Attorney Linda Dunikoski.

"Yes," replied Thandiwe.

Taleeb Starkes referred to the case with, "Alternatively, had this urban terrorist been a bloodthirsty White supremacist who mercilessly killed two unsuspecting Black women, Negro-geddon would have commenced."

"Racial resentment is the new mother's milk of education," said a prison psychologist at the trial who did not wish to be identified. "Students, black and white, learn from their earliest days that blacks are victims and powerless to fight racism, not just in school, but also in churches and from their parents. The attitude of victimization breeds resentment and violence. But most dangerous of all, black students are taught they are not responsible for their behavior because they are the victims of white racism," he said. "I see that every day in the prison where I work."

Even so, victimization remains the bread and butter of today's black leadership. There appears to be no sensibility or compassion to the true victims of their teachings. In Wilmington, Del., the pastor of one of the largest black congregations in the state said: "This violence in our community, you don't think it has something to do with the last 400 years?"

Rev. Lawrence M. Livingston, black Pastor of Mother African Union Church in Wilmington, Delaware, helped young blacks to justify delinquency by stating, "We didn't create this stuff – all this mess." In other words, the problem traces back to white racism, not black delinquency. The comment was in response to a mob of blacks beating a white clergyman near Livingston's church.

The message of black victimization is now written in stone and there is a fear among the media to report black crime for the fear of damaging the black community at large. Editors for the Los Angeles Times and the Chicago Tribune have admitted censoring black crimes. The motive was "to protect blacks from being stigmatized.

18-year-old Carter Strange decided to go jogging at night in Columbia, South Carolina. At the same time, a group of eight black youths, aged 13-18, were busy hunting for a white person to attack. When they nearly beat Strange to death, it took four days for the attack to draw media attention.

Not long after, Philadelphia police said that a mob of 50 to 100 blacks roamed the streets and finally assaulted a half dozen whites.

In none of these cases did the press call the attacks a hate crime. In none did the police charge the offenders with a hate crime. If going to the streets in search of a person of a different color is not a hate crime, one must wonder what the new definition is.

I have called the mounting wave of black violence an epidemic and the term could not be more correct. The trend is no longer simply robberies or assaults in search of money, but it's purposely targeting white people and committing atrocities in the process.

At the age of 23, six foot tall, blonde-haired and blue-eyed Andrew Schreiber had reason to be pleased with his life. He had always been an outdoors type so his job as assistant baseball coach at Newman University in Wichita, Kansas, suited him perfectly. He says he has been a baseball enthusiast "since I could walk. I usually play catcher so I can be involved in every play, every pitch." When he's not catching a ball on a diamond field, he's often putting one on a golf course.

On the chilly night of December 8, 2000, the strapping bachelor feared his life would come to an abrupt end.

He was at a Kum & Go convenience store when two young black men approached him and brandished a gun. They ordered him into his own car. As his heart hammered, the men told him to drive to various ATMs where they forced him to withdraw $800. Later Schreiber said, "I was just hoping if I did what they said, they'd let me live."

They did. The assailants released him in a field, physically unharmed but badly shaken. They shot out the tires of his vehicle, then jumped in another car and sped away.

Schreiber had no way of knowing that he was the first victim in a crime spree of escalating violence that would culminate in a night of grotesque violence aptly called the "Wichita Horror."

The next victim of that crime spree was fair-skinned, bespectacled, and red-haired Ann Walenta. A youthful-looking 55-year-old, she was a cellist and librarian with the

Wichita Symphony Orchestra. As orchestra librarian, she was responsible for ordering and keeping track of its music.

Classical music was the great love of Walenta's life, coming just after her husband and two grown children. It was a love she enjoyed bringing to others, which was one reason she had worked for a group that taught classical music to young black people.

Walenta and her husband lived in a comfortable single-story dwelling in a quiet, upscale neighborhood, the kind people move to hoping to avoid crime. At about 9:30 p.m. on the cold, dry night of December 11, she returned home after a rehearsal with the Wichita Symphony Orchestra and parked her sport-utility vehicle in front of her house.

A man approached her. "I need some help," he said. Then he pulled a gun and ordered, "Don't move the car!"

The panicked woman started to drive away but gunfire shattered the glass of the car window and ripped through her body. Severely wounded but still conscious, she pressed her car's horn. Its incessant blare drew the attention of a neighbor who called 911.

Walenta survived for several days. She recovered consciousness and spoke with police from her hospital bed before dying of her injuries. While she was still clinging to life, her murderers would commit an even greater outrage.

It was snowing on the night of December 14, 2000, when 25-year-old schoolteacher H.G. (she is identified only by her initials in deference to the custom protecting the privacy of living sex crime victims) slid behind the wheel of her red Toyota Paseo. Her dear schnauzer, Nikki, sat beside her on the passenger seat.

H.G. looked forward to a pleasant evening with close friends and a night with the man she loved. That man was bespectacled and handsome Jason Befort, 26, who taught science at Augusta High School and coached the boys' junior varsity basketball team. He was a popular teacher with a flamboyant streak expressed in the bright blue shoes he habitually wore.

Befort shared a triplex with two other young men, Brad Heyka, 27, and Aaron Sander, 29. Heyka worked for petroleum and chemical conglomerate Koch Industries, where he was a valued employee thought to have a bright future. The chubby man with the winning smile and lively sense of humor had earned three promotions in as many years.

Sander was a slender, fresh-faced man who looked younger than his years. A devout Roman Catholic, he had recently quit Koch because he felt called to the priesthood.

H.G. arrived at her beau's 12727 Birchwood Dr. home at about 8:30 p.m. Having her own key, she let herself inside the condominium. She saw Heyka and Sander but not Befort.

First Heather Muller, 25, then Befort, joined the group. Muller was a pretty woman who wore her light brown hair in a pageboy and attended graduate school at Wichita State University. She and Sander had dated, drawn to each other in part because of their shared commitment to the Roman Catholic Church. That piety had also led to their recent break-up as a couple since Sander wanted to enter the priesthood. They remained close friends and Muller was starting to feel that, like Sander, she might have a religious vocation and spoke of becoming a nun.

Befort was in love with H. G. and wanted to marry her but had not yet worked up the nerve to "pop the question." He had recently bought an engagement ring for her and, at the same time, purchased a book on how to propose.

The five friends watched TV, ate dinner, and made conversation before heading off to their various beds.

Befort and H.G. were snuggling together under the sheets when the porch light suddenly came on. "Don't tell me I have to get up and turn off the light again," Befort said irritably.

H.G. heard Sander talking with someone. The voices were muffled so she assumed he was chatting with Muller. H.G. turned to look at the digital clock and could not make it out completely because her boyfriend's head was in the way but saw that it was sometime after 11:00 p.m.

The bedroom was in semi-darkness when its door burst open. Befort screamed.

A tall black male pointing a gun stood in the doorway. He came into the room and tore the covers off the bed in which H.G. and Jason were lying. Then a second black man, also armed with a gun, led Sander into the room.

Since the room was cloaked in darkness, it was hard for H.G. to physically differentiate between the intruders except to see that the second man was not as tall or thickly built as the first. The shorter man shoved Sander onto the bed.

Little Nikki growled and bared her teeth.

"Grab your dog," one of the invaders said, "or we'll shoot her."

"Who else is here?" the other man demanded. The terrified victims told of Heyka and Muller. One of the attackers headed down the stairs while the other guarded H.G., Befort, and Sander.

Clad in a white undershirt and a pair of boxers, Heyka was brought up into the bedroom. The intruder then left, retrieved a fully clothed Muller and brought her to the room.

"Get undressed!" an intruder ordered.

All five took their clothes off.

The shorter man left his partner to guard the victims while he checked out the house.

"Do you have any money?" the taller gunman asked the now-naked group.

Eager to cooperate, the desperate victims begged him to "take our money!"

He asked who had ATM cards. Each victim raised a hand and told him the amount. Lights were switched on in the living room area.

"Where's the safe?" the taller man asked.

The men who lived there said there was no safe and the robber replied, "In a house this nice there has to be a safe!"

The shorter man returned to the room. Muller and H.G. were ordered to go to the wet bar area located just outside Jason's bedroom.

A hideous sexual orgy began. The women were commanded to perform oral sex and digital penetration on each other. Then Muller was taken back to the bedroom and Heyka ordered into the wet bar where he was told to have sexual intercourse with H.G. Unable to get an erection, he forced his soft penis into her.

The intruder expressed anger over Heyka's inability to get an erection.

Heyka was told to stop, then led out of the room. Befort was brought into the wet bar and ordered to have intercourse with H.G. He pushed his flaccid organ into her vagina.

Then one of the intruders said, "That's his girl. Don't let him do it with his girl."

He was returned to the bedroom and Sander brought into the wet bar and told to have sex with H.G. "I can't do it," he pleaded. They told him he had to and one of them hit him in the back of the head with the butt of his gun.

Sander pushed his limp penis into H.G.'s vagina and went through the motions of intercourse.

The attackers directed H.G. to leave the bar area. She accompanied them back to the bedroom. They ordered her into the closet where she joined Befort and Heyka. The victims were told not to speak. The folding doors of the closet were shut on three naked, frightened people.

Muller and Sander were commanded to go to enter the wet bar.

The intruders again ordered Sander to get an erection and again he said he could not. He was told he had until 11:54 to "get hard." The angry captor counted the minutes from 11:52 to 11:54.

When the time was up, the man beat Sander, probably with a golf club from the residence.

They took Sander to the closet and ordered Befort out of it. During that time, H.G. could hear Muller moaning in pain. Some minutes passed and Befort was brought back to the closet.

The intruders led Heyka out of the closet and ordered him to have intercourse with Muller.

When he was brought back to the closet, the attackers told the victims they were going to ATM machines to withdraw funds. The victims were allowed out of the closet and told to get their car keys. In their confusion, Heyka, H.G., and Muller were unable to find them. Angered, the captors threatened to "pop" someone unless they located their keys.

Befort found the keys to his silver Dodge Dakota truck atop the entertainment center in his room.

H.G. was able to see the intruders more clearly. The taller man wore a black coat she thought was made of leather. He also had black leather gloves on his hands. The shorter man had what she called "poofy" hair styled in clumps.

Befort was ordered to dress and accompany the taller man while the shorter guarded the other four.

The captor staying behind ordered H. G. to prepare herself for sex. She complied, masturbating to try to get her vagina lubricated. While she was on the floor, she heard him unzipping his pants and saw his gun lying about two feet away from her. Her hand itched to grab it but she feared she would not be quick enough to get it before he could. Having little experience with firearms, she was uncertain she would even be able to shoot it. She thought he might take it away from her and kill her right then so she did not take the chance. H.G. had made up her mind that no matter what humiliations she had to endure, she was going to survive this ordeal if it was at all possible.

She was raped for about five minutes. Then he took her back to the closet and brought Muller out of it. The captives obeyed the order not to talk but Sander could not help weeping as he heard Muller's pained moans.

The taller man returned to the house with Befort in tow. Befort was ordered to strip again. In the closet, for the first time, a tearful Sander disobeyed the order not to speak to his fellow victims. He whispered to Heyka: "Do you think they're going to kill us?" Heyka did not respond.

Heyka was allowed to dress, then taken from the home.

When he was brought back, the taller man opened the closet door and asked, "Who's next?"

H. G. stood up. Sander said, "No, I'll go." But he sat down when H.G. continued making preparations for her trip. She was not permitted to get fully dressed as the men had been but was allowed to put on only a sweater. She walked into the freezing night naked from the waist down, her bare feet in the snow.

The kidnapper escorted her to Befort's truck. Without speaking, he waved a gloved hand at the driver's side door to indicate that she should drive. She backed the truck out of the icy driveway and turned towards 127th Street.

He asked her what his crime partner had done with her and she said he had forced her to have sex with him.

The captor laughed. "Did you like it?" he asked.

"Yes," the victim replied, hoping not to anger him.

He asked if she had ever been with a black man before and H.G. said she had not. Then he asked if the rapist was "better" than her boyfriend was. Again she said, "yes."

Did she like being with a girl? He wanted to know.

"No," she replied.

"Baby, that's all right," he said, "you ain't got to lie to me."

H.G. drove without speaking, then blurted out, "Are you going to shoot us?"

"No," he replied.

"You know," a desperate H.G. continued, "you can have whatever you want. Please don't hurt us. Do you promise you're not going to shoot us or kill us?"

"Yeah," he said.

She stopped the truck in front of a drive-up ATM machine then rolled the window down on her side of the vehicle and started to use her card to withdraw money. The man put his gloved hand on her sex organ and rubbed. Startled, H.G. fell against the window. When she recovered her balance, she handed him the money.

Then she drove in silence while he channel surfed the radio.

Sometime during the trip, he told H.G. he wished the two had met under different circumstances. He said she was cute and he thought the two of them would have hit it off.

"Yeah, me too," she said.

He swore when asking her what she meant.

"Well, I'm not really having a good time," she explained honestly.

H.G. parked the truck in the driveway at 12727 Birchwood Dr. The pair walked back into the house. He ordered Sander to accompany him.

Muller was sitting on the floor by the wet bar area. She was the only one of the victims who would not be taken to an ATM that night. H.G. did not make eye contact with

Muller but remembered her as looking "spaced out, shocked."

After the shorter captor walked H.G. to the closet and put her in with Heyka and Befort, he shut the door on the three.

"What is Weller's?" he asked Muller.

"It's whiskey," she replied.

There were the sounds of a drink being made. The closet door opened and the intruder asked if anyone wanted a drink. All three said they did not. He had found a muzzle for Nikki in her basket under the sink and threw that in the closet. H.G. put it on her dog as he shut the closet door.

There were sounds like a jug full of change being shaken. The captor asked, "Whose is this?"

Muller told him it was probably H.G.'s but "she doesn't know about it yet."

It was the diamond ring with which Befort had planned to surprise her.

Eventually Sander and the other captor returned to the home.

The taller captor summoned H.G. from the closet and took her to the dining room. He noticed her earrings. "What are those?" he asked.

"They're fake," she said. "You know, you can have them if you want them." She pulled them off her ears.

"No, I don't want them," he replied.

She left the earrings on top of a stack of boxes containing Christmas decorations.

Then he said something she could not remember but that scared her, causing her to jerk.

"Relax," he said. "We're not going to shoot you yet."

Terror seized her at this betrayal of the promise of not shooting them at all.

He ordered her to get down on all fours. Then he raped her, first vaginally and then orally.

After these rapes, the man made H.G. accompany him to the bathroom where his partner was raping Muller. "Hold on," the rapist in the bathroom said, "I'm not done."

When he was "done," he indicated with a motion that H.G. should come into the bathroom with him. Then he raped her. For the first time, H.G. noticed that the shorter man was wearing a black leather jacket, an orange and black FUBU sweater, jeans, and tan hiking boots.

After this rape, H.G. thought he might have removed a condom although she never saw it but only heard him flush the toilet.

Then the women were directed to exit the bathroom and go to the area of the wet bar and sit on the floor. The invaders spoke softly between themselves. The taller man went downstairs, then came back up. The two whispered again and H.G. made out the words "big screen."

The captors ordered Muller and H.G., both of whom were shoeless and naked below the waist, to leave the house for the garage. There they were told to get into the trunk of Sander's Honda Accord. The nude male victims were brought out and also ordered into the small trunk but not all five would fit. The attackers told the men to get into the trunk and the women into the back seat of the car.

Muller looked at H.G. and said, "I wonder how long they can last in a trunk."

The garage door opened and the criminals talked with each other. The taller man told H.G. to get out of Sander's car and accompany him to Befort's truck. The shorter man got into the driver's seat of Sander's vehicle.

After the taller kidnapper had been driving for awhile, H.G. asked him where they were going.

He replied that they wanted to drop the victims off away from either the attackers' car or their own cars. Eventually both kidnappers parked in a snow covered soccer field.

The trunk of the Honda Accord was opened. Befort, Sander, and Heyka were told to kneel in front of the car.

Panicked, H.G. looked at Muller and cried, "They're going to shoot us!"

Both women were commanded to kneel beside the men.

A gun fired and Sander begged, "Please, no, sir, please!"

The gun fired again and H.G. felt a bullet slam into her head. She remembered that her mind "went kind of gray with white like stars" but she was not knocked unconscious. Someone kicked her from behind and she fell forward. She lay in the snow, pretending to be dead in the hope that they would not hurt her anymore.

The truck started and ran over the victims. H.G. suffered its terrible impact but still did not lose consciousness. Then she heard the truck start yet again and believed from the way the sound traveled that it was leaving the area. She turned her head slightly and saw that she was correct.

Still lying in the snow, the wounded woman called out the names of her lover and her friends. "Jason? Heather? Aaron? Brad?"

Victims, J. Befort, H. Muller, A. Sander, B. Heyka, clockwise

No one answered.

H. G. waited until she could no longer make out the truck's headlights. Then she got up to examine the other victims who lay exposed and face down in the snow.

Befort was next to her. She rolled his naked and battered body over. This was the man she loved, the man she knew loved her. He wanted to marry her but had not gotten the chance to slip the engagement ring on her finger.

Blood flowed from his head and eyes. Maybe he was still alive! Shivering and near-naked, H.G. removed her sweater, the only garment she had on, and tied it around his head to stop the bleeding.

She went to Heyka but soon realized there was not much she could do to help while she was there.

Seeing lights to the west a ways off, she thought the building that had them "was like some sort of farming type thing" and believed it might not have a phone. Looking toward the highway, she saw a home with Christmas lights on.

Like all things identified with this holiday season, bright and multi-colored Christmas lights represent joy and love and the spirit of giving.

For H. G., from whom so much had been taken — loved ones, security, and dignity — those lights meant comfort and help.

As she raced toward the Christmas lights, she saw car headlights and immediately dove into the frigid blanket of snow because she feared it might be the attackers. Every time she saw headlights, she flung herself to the ground, waited, then got back up to run toward those beckoning lights.

H.G. got to a fence and climbed over it. She crossed a highway that was almost empty due to the hour. Then she climbed over another fence and found herself on a dirt road that appeared to be behind a subdivision. She got to the back of a home, then raced around to the front door and repeatedly rang the doorbell and pounded on the door.

She had run a mile. As a child, H.G. was nicknamed "Toughy" by her playmates. She had lived up to that name.

The owners of the home, a man and a woman, peeked out a window to see a shivering, bleeding, naked woman on their porch.

They opened the door and let her inside, then bundled her up in blankets.

"Call 911!" H.G. exclaimed.

The man made the call. First he tried to tell the police emergency operator what H.G. had told him. Then he handed her the phone. Somehow H. G. was able to make herself speak clearly and calmly as she directed the police to the soccer field. She hoped that Befort might still be alive.

He was not. H.G.'s hopes were dashed and her heart broken when told that the man she loved and three people dear to her were found dead.

Police believe that while H.G. was making her way painfully through the snow, the attackers returned to the 12727 Birchwood Dr. house to steal more items. They also beat and stabbed H.G.'s muzzled dog Nikki to death.

Wichita TV stations filled with stories of the grisly quadruple homicide. One of those news reports led to the first break in the case. On the morning after the slayings, Christian Taylor watched a broadcast on which he heard a description of Jason Befort's truck. Taylor believed a truck he had seen parked at his apartment complex could be Befort's and went to a police substation to report his suspicion. Police rushed to the apartment complex where they identified the truck in question as Befort's.

Another resident of that same apartment complex, Riwa Obel Nsangalufu, flagged down some police officers to tell them he had helped a man carry a large screen TV to an apartment. He pointed them to that second story apartment.

Police swooped down on that apartment, then knocked on the door. The tall black man inside it went onto the porch and put a leg up on the railing as if to jump from it. However, he saw that it was surrounded by law enforcement and returned back inside. Stephanie Donley, his pretty, white, dark-haired girlfriend, opened the door. Police entered, clapped the handcuffs on the suspect's wrists and read him his rights.

He was Reginald Carr, 22, from Dodge City. Accompanied by his younger brother Jonathan, 20, he had recently arrived in Wichita. The elder Carr had an extensive arrest record while the younger had a less serious one. Both had only worked intermittently at legitimate jobs.

News of Reginald's arrest was broadcast on TV that afternoon. To one of those watching, Andrew Schreiber, that face was sickeningly familiar. Schreiber phoned police to say he thought Reginald was one of the men who had robbed him.

Authorities believed Reginald was the man described by H.G. as the taller and heavier of the two attackers.

Then police got their second big break.

Toni Green is the mother of Tronda Adams, a young woman Jonathan Carr had been courting for about a week. That morning had not started out well for Greene. At her job as a home health care professional, she felt queasy and left. When she got home, she recovered enough to do a bit of housekeeping. Soon she had an eerie sense about the man sleeping on her couch. The news description of a suspect in a mass murder sounded awfully like him. She picked up Jonathan's leather jacket and found a little jewelry box with a diamond ring in it. Greene knew it could not be for her daughter whom Jonathan had just met. News reports said the robbers at the multiple homicide had stolen a diamond ring. Green also remembered that authorities were looking for a Plymouth that figured in the crimes. Her daughter's new boyfriend had parked a white Plymouth in front of her home.

It had to be the same man, Green decided. She whispered these fears to her daughter and told her to grab the niece who was staying with them and get out of the house. Since snow was on the ground, Adams wanted to get her shoes first.

"You can leave without your shoes," a frantic Greene urged. "Let's go!"

As they crossed the street, Greene called 911 on her cell phone. "The guy you're looking for is at my house," she told the operator.

The three females ran to the home of Dawnyieka Buggs across the street. When Greene, Adams, and the niece got there, they turned around to see Jonathan Carr standing on Greene's porch in jeans and a t-shirt.

He ran.

Police were on the scene almost immediately and gave chase. They caught up with him two blocks from Green's home, hiding between a house's storm door and front door. The arresting officers found over $1,000 in cash on him. He had lost a shoe while running.

At the time of the Carrs' arrest, Ann Walenta was still alive in the hospital. Police showed her a photographic line-up that included the Carr brothers. The dying woman picked out Reginald as the man who shot her. She pointed to another man who rang a bell of familiarity. He was not Jonathan but a man in prison at the time.

With the Carr brothers in custody, authorities secured a search warrant for DNA testing. A nurse took samples of hair, blood, and saliva.

As Jonathan Carr awaited the sampling, he spoke to homicide detective Kelly Otis. Jonathan apparently remembered the Dec. 7, 2000 case of another Wichita quadruple murder in which four teenagers were shot and two men arrested for those crimes. Both victims and suspects were black.

"What happened to those boys who shot those kids?" Jonathan asked.

"They've been charged with capital murder," Otis replied.

"What's capital murder?"

"Well, anyone convicted of capital murder," Otis explained, "can get the death penalty."

"How's that done?" Jonathan queried.

"Lethal injection," the detective said.

There was a long pause. Then Jonathan asked, "Do you feel anything [from that]?"

"We've never been able to ask anyone," Otis replied.

Wichita was in torment. In the space of a week, the city had been the scene of two unrelated quadruple murders. Although suspects in both mass slayings were in custody, purchases of guns, locks, and security systems skyrocketed.

A fierce debate raged in the media and among the citizenry about the motive for the Wichita Horror. Rick Thames, editor of the *Wichita Eagle*, said, "It was a shocking crime because of the apparent randomness of it."

Others argued that the crime was not random but racist. They blasted the decision of Sedgwick County District Attorney Nola Foulston not to treat it as a "hate crime." She contended that there was no evidence race was the motive. No racial slurs were made against any of the victims. Foulston maintained that robbery was at the root of these crimes, Kansas does not have a hate-crimes statute on the books. However, it does have a special penalty provision allowing increased sentences for crimes motivated by racial hatred. On many other grounds, but not that one, the prosecution sought the death penalty against the Carrs.

Some observers protested that if a similar outrage had been perpetrated against blacks by whites, it would have been *assumed* to be racist. The question asked of H.G. about whether or not she had previously had sex with a black man suggests race was on his mind.

Sadly, white racists attempted to foment hatred because of this case. In the aftermath of the slayings, online white supremacist and separatist groups put up web pages detailing the offenses and decrying what they saw as the media's double standard in giving them relatively little attention.

However, a commentator does not have to be a white racist or even white to wonder if a similar white-on-black mass murder would have gotten more press attention. The concern that decent Americans have with ending racism, together with the history of white dominance in this country, may make the media reluctant to focus on cases that threaten to bring the old racial poisons to the surface. The respected black conservative author Thomas Sowell claims that the media has a double standard regarding inter-racial offenses, tending to play up "vicious crimes by whites against blacks" but play down equally "vicious crimes by blacks against whites."

A similar controversy occurred when the homophobic murder of Mathew Shepherd was closely followed by the murder of Jessie Dirkhising. Shepherd was viciously beaten to death in a gay-bashing incident. Two gay men raped 13-year-old Jessie Dirkhising with a variety of implements. He died as a result. The Shepherd case was far more widely publicized than the Dirkhising homicide and some blasted the media, alleging that they showed a pro-gay bias in giving so much more attention to one death than the other. However, the story of the boy's death got prominent play on anti-homosexual websites.

The Wichita Horror also figured in accusations Kansas politicians flung at their foes. In October 2001, state representative Tony Powell, who was considering a run for attorney general, accused the sitting attorney general, David Adkins, of contributing to the murders by supporting a bill that cut the amount of time convicts stayed under parole supervision.

That law benefited Reginald Carr, who had been on parole for aggravated assault and drug charges, by cutting his parole term from two years to one. However, his parole term had been incorrectly terminated six months before it should have ended even with the new law due to a paperwork error.

Despite that mistake, Powell said, "I hold people like (Mr.) Adkins responsible for what happened" and asserted that the bill "arguably led to the execution-style killings."

An outraged Adkins retorted, "This is more of a despicable reflection on his [Powell's] character and doesn't take into account an understanding of the law or the facts of the case."

In July 2002, television advertisements appeared on Wichita stations invoking the case to support Phil Kline in his race for the Republican nomination for Kansas ' attorney general attorney against David Adkins. Incredibly, the ad stated as fact that Reginald Carr committed murders with which he was only charged!

Kline's campaign disavowed advance knowledge of the ad and TV stations pulled it the next day. A supposedly non-partisan anti-crime group called The Law Enforcement Alliance of America had sponsored the bizarre commercial.

Reginald and Jonathan were charged with 113 crimes, including five counts of capital murder and multiple counts of rape and robbery. They were also charged with animal cruelty.

Judge Paul Clark presided over the trial.

Chief deputy district attorney Kim Parker assisted Nola Foulston in the prosecution.

The lead attorney for Reginald Carr was Jay Greeno who is often recognized by his neat ponytail of gray hair. A public defender for ten years, he has been in private practice since 1994. Val Wachtel was Greeno's co-counsel.

Looking something like an "odd couple," slim and clean shaven Mark Manna and heavyset and bearded Ron Evans were the lawyers for Jonathan Carr.

Prosecution and defense questioned prospective jurors on a variety of issues, including feelings about race, the death penalty, and what they had read and heard about the Wichita Horror. The court excused three people because they had been friends of one or more of the victims. One man was excused because he strongly opposed the death penalty.

Seven men and five women, two blacks and ten whites were impaneled as the jury. The group included an accountant, a machinist, an unemployed woman, an executive, a carpenter, and a nurse.

Much of the testimony was grisly. The most riveting witness was undoubtedly H.G., who was called to the stand early in the trial. She described the ordeal of rape that she and her friends had endured, the way they were robbed at ATMs, and finally the brutal shootings. Her testimony was much as it had been in the preliminary hearing with one vital exception. She identified Reginald Carr as the taller of the attackers and indicated that her previous failure to identify him was due to his having shaved his head and donned glasses.

Amazingly, evidence put on by prosecutor Foulston showed that H.G.'s life had been saved by a hair clip! Experts testified that such a clip had deflected the bullet from her head.

Police Department Crime Scene Investigator Barbara Siwek told the court that H.G.'s dog, Nikki, had been beaten, possibly with a golf club, and then stabbed by an ice pick.

Trauma surgeon Scott Porter testified to the injuries suffered by Ann Walenta and used an anatomical mannequin to show the jury where she was shot. His unavoidably graphic description led to courtroom drama when a 51-year-old juror fainted. Dr. Porter left the stand to attend to the distressed juror. The juror soon regained consciousness but was taken to a hospital and examined. He made a full recovery and went back on the jury.

Sedgwick County coroner Mary Dudley testified about wounds suffered by the victims. She told the somber courtroom that Heather Muller and Aaron Sander were shot with the gun actually touching their heads. The shooter had been slightly farther away from Brad Heyka and Jason Befort. The examination of Muller's body showed she had been raped. All three male victims had bruises on their bodies. The injuries could have been made by a golf club like that found in the home.

On cross-examination, Jonathan's attorney, Mark Manna, asked if the distances between shooter and victim indicated that only one person did the killing. The coroner said she could not know that.

Andrew Schreiber took the stand and told the jury how he had been kidnapped, robbed, and then left in a field. He identified Reginald Carr as one of the two men who abducted him but could not identify Jonathan Carr. Under cross-examination, Schreiber admitted that he had been unable to identify either brother from a photo lineup soon after the events.

The prosecutors put on many exhibits and called numerous witnesses to physically link the Carrs to the crimes.

They filled the courtroom with items belonging to the victims that were discovered in the apartment of Reginald

Carr. Among them were two TVs including a big-screen Sony, a VCR, a CD player, and a 120-piece tool set still in its package. Other stolen goods displayed were three remote controls, a cordless phone, power cords, drinking glasses, dress shoes, jackets, and coats. Relatives and friends of the victims testified that property displayed as that of the victims had belonged to them.

More technical evidence tied the brothers to the crimes.

Forensic investigator Gary Miller, a florid man with a mustache and thinning hair, matched a shoe imprint on a windshield sunshade recovered from the 12727 Birchwood Dr. garage floor to the shoe Jonathan lost while fleeing police. He also linked bullets from the gun used to shoot out the tires of Andrew Schreiber's car and kill Walenta and cartridges found at the 12727 E. Birchwood Dr. residence to a single gun by firing markings on bullets and cartridges. However, that gun had been found discarded near an off-ramp a few blocks from the soccer field in which the victims were shot. Miller could not directly connect that firearm, a .380-caliber black Lorcin pistol, to either Reginald or Jonathan.

Sidney Schueler, a DNA expert for the Kansas Bureau of Investigation, testified that Jonathan Carr's DNA was found in a semen spot on the carpet of the Birchwood home and on swabs taken from H.G. He said that blood spots found on Reginald's clothing were originally from Heather Muller.

Reginald Carr's lawyers suggested the drops could have gotten there by his having rubbed against someone else — like Jonathan.

Women who had known and cared about the Carrs took the stand against them.

Tronda Adams testified she met Reginald and Jonathan early the evening of Dec. 7, 2000, the night Andrew Schreiber was kidnapped. Adams said she saw Jonathan Carr regularly. He visited her late Dec. 11, approximately one hour after Ann Walenta was shot and handed Adams a black semi-automatic handgun which she kept until he retrieved it from her before Dec. 14. When he took the gun back, he meticulously cleaned it. She said both brothers visited her Dec. 14, the night of the multiple homicides, and left around 9:00 p.m. Jonathan phoned her 3:31 a.m. the next morning.

Adams ' mother, Toni Greene, took the stand to recount how she started to suspect Jonathan after a news report and had her suspicions heightened by the discovery of the diamond ring. She told of herself, her daughter, and a niece racing across the street and making the 911 call that led to Jonathan's arrest.

Reginald's girlfriend, Stephanie Donley, testified that she believed neither Reginald nor Jonathan was employed but that Reginald was carrying large amounts of cash in early December 2000. He explained his sudden fortune by saying his pit bull was winning fights. She said she allowed the Carr brothers to borrow her Toyota Camry at about 5:30 p.m. Dec. 14th and that they brought it back about twelve hours later. Her testimony connected Reginald to possessions stolen from the victims when she said he moved several items into her home which were identified as belonging to them.

The saddest part of her testimony linked Reginald and H. G. in a sickeningly intimate way. A nurse, Donley said she recognized a sexually transmitted disease, genital warts, on her boyfriend's private parts early in their relationship. A medical expert would later testify that H. G. had come down with genital warts.

On Oct. 25th, 2002, after putting 849 exhibits into evidence, the state rested its case against Jonathan and Reginald Carr.

In the face of that mountain of evidence, the defense looked pitifully weak.

Jonathan Carr's attorneys pinned his case on a ticket; and an unused ticket at that. In his opening statement, Mark Manna told the jury that his client had planned to catch a train at the time of the quadruple homicide but got lost leaving Wichita. They entered that Amtrak train ticket, dated the morning of the murders, into evidence, then rested.

Lawyers for Reginald Carr failed to get their major evidence admitted. Reginald wanted to take the stand to claim that Jonathan had told him he had been with a man who was "tripping" and "shooting people." He also wanted to say he moved the loot from the robberies into Donley's apartment to help his brother who was involved in the crimes along with the unknown partner.

The judge ruled such testimony would be inadmissible hearsay.

Val Wachtel tried to enter into evidence medical records he said would suggest that Ann Walenta died due to medical malpractice. The judge denied the request.

Strangely, Reginald's attorneys had the police interview with H.G. re-played for the jury. They did not give a reason but observers believed they wished to emphasize the vagueness of her description of Reginald.

Some of the jurors appeared distressed as the tape played. H.G. left the courtroom.

DNA expert Jami Harman took the stand for Reginald. She pointed out that since Reginald and Jonathan are brothers, DNA taken from H.G. could not be said with certainty to come from both of them. On cross-examination, Harmon conceded that blood stains on Reginald's clothes were those of Heather Muller.

In closing argument, prosecutor Kim Parker told the jury, "This is a crime driven by greed and lust, by selfishness and driven by twisted sexual gratification."

In their summations, defense attorneys for each Carr brother pointed fingers at the other. Wachtel emphasized that there were inconsistencies in witness identification and noted that DNA at the crime scene belonged to Jonathan rather than Reginald.

Mark Manna reminded that jury that both Ann Walenta and Andrew Schreiber had identified Reginald but not Jonathan. Reginald was the one found with most of the belongings stolen that night, Manna elaborated. "Reginald Carr was not alone," Manna said, "but the evidence will show who was playing the lead role that night — directing things, taking things. . . . Don't just go back there and check the box guilty on all counts, please consider [Jonathan's] guilt and innocence separate from damning evidence against his brother, Reginald."

On Nov. 4, 2002, the jury returned its verdicts. Jonathan and Reginald were convicted on almost all counts. Those convictions included multiple counts of capital murder, aggravated kidnapping, aggravated robbery, and rape. They were convicted of raping the male as well as the female victims. The jury did not forget little Nikki and found both brothers guilty of animal cruelty. Jonathan was acquitted on four counts of the kidnapping and robbery of Andrew Schreiber.

The defendants looked stoical as the verdicts were read.

Relatives of the victims seemed relieved. They hugged each other as well as people involved in the investigation and prosecution.

Now the question for the jury to decide was what punishment to fix for the heinous crimes.

A disturbing incident occurred in the city during the penalty phase. A Wichita resident hung the Carr brothers in effigy in his front yard. The spectacle of two dark-faced dummies hanging from trees with ropes around their necks outraged many who saw it as reminiscent of the notorious lynchings of black men. Rev. Gill Ford, NAACP regional director in Denver, Colorado, was informed of the display by the Wichita NAACP and said the noose is to blacks "like the swastika to somebody who's been in a concentration camp. My hope is that the community of Wichita as a whole would condemn those kinds of actions."

Michael Watley, a black carpet layer in Wichita, was disgusted by the display but hoped it did not represent a strong undercurrent of racism in his city. "I know there is some prejudice here," he explained, "but I didn't think it was to that level." He added that he has no sympathy for Jonathan and Reginald Carr. "They're individuals," he pointed out, "and it doesn't matter about skin color. What they did, they did on their own."

After many complaints, the resident took the effigies down. He claimed he was not thinking of the possible racial ramifications of the display but merely wanted to express his repugnance for the crimes of the Carrs.

During the penalty phase, attorneys for the Carrs put on witnesses to describe their formative years. They painted a picture of childhoods bereft of normal affection in an unstable and violent family.

Janice Harding, the mother of Jonathan and Reginald, said her sons grew up without warmth and intimacy. "I'm not a huggy, kissy person," she admitted. The family celebrated no holidays. It suffered a terrible trauma when a daughter, Regina, died of leukemia when she was only 3.

She said Jonathan and Reginald's father turned violent when they quarreled. "Their dad used to hit me," she claimed. She was also violent to him and once, "I picked up a bat up [sic] and beat him with it. I told him he wasn't going to hit me again."

When she and the boys' father divorced, he completely dropped out of his sons' lives. Her second marriage was also violent and her husband once put a gun to her head. Occasionally Jonathan and Reginald lived with their maternal grandmother but that environment was not much of an improvement. "She flips out," Harding commented. "One minute she's normal, the next she's yelling and screaming."

Harding said she sympathized with what her sons' victims' families were going through: "I feel for the other families. Everybody's hurting right now." Then she spoke directly to her sons in the defendants' dock. "I don't know what went wrong but I love you," she said. "I'm sorry if I did something wrong. I'm sorry."

Reginald and Jonathan's oldest sister testified to a childhood marred by sexual as well as physical abuse. She said her father sexually abused her and her mother's boyfriends sexually molested her brothers.

The sister described how emotional damage manifested itself. Reginald was a fighter in school. Jonathan attempted suicide by drinking antifreeze when he was sixteen.

She said Reginald told her that he shot all four victims in the soccer field. Under cross-examination, she admitted that, in the past, Reginald sometimes took blame to shield Jonathan.

Forensic psychologist Thomas Reidy testified that Reginald's experiences with sex, drugs, and violence began at age 6. He was still in the first years of elementary school when he was sexually abused and found pornographic photographs that featured his mother. Discipline in the Carr household was harsh. Their mother administered corporal punishment with electrical cords. When he was 11, Reginald was given liquor and drugs by older relatives. As

Ron Sylvester reported in *The Wichita Eagle*, "Reidy found that Reginald Carr attended eight schools from kindergarten through eighth grade. By then, he had sexually harassed a teacher on one of the days he bothered showing up. He was absent 32 days that year.

"During his freshman year in high school at Dodge City, Reginald earned 21 detentions and suspensions. After beating up a student, he dropped out of ninth grade, Reidy testified, before the school could kick him out." He was in prison by 18.

Forensic psychologist Mark Cunningham described Jonathan Carr's upbringing as combining the "five Hs: hopeless, helpless, homeless, hungry, and hug-less." That childhood left him and his brother "so void of empathy and attachment that they could do this to other young people."

On cross-examination, prosecutor Parker repeatedly drew out Cunningham's admission that Jonathan Carr does understand the difference between right and wrong.

"There is no question," the psychologist said, "he has awareness of wrongful behavior."

"He doesn't care," Parker asserted.

"That's correct," Cunningham answered.

Dr. David Preston, a peer reviewer of the *Journal of Nuclear Medicine*, testified to a possible physical factor in the men's criminality. He said that both Reginald and Jonathan have brain damage to their temporal lobes, the part of the brain that involves risk evaluation and short-term memory.

The mothers of Reginald Carr's children took the stand. His estranged wife Mandy Carr said his relationship with his children is weak and told of the painful awkwardness of trying to explain the situation their father is in to them.

Richelle Kossman has a seven-year-old son by Reginald. While Reginald did not support the boy financially, he often visited and was a caring father to him. Kossman read a letter that her son wrote to his dad when Reginald was in jail: "I wish you would come back. I love you very, very much. I love when you play games with me . . . I'm a good boy like you tell me."

Usually expressionless, Reginald bowed his head as his son's letter was read to the courtroom.

One witness tried to show a positive side to Jonathan Carr. Juanita Culver said she and her husband had hired Jonathan to do carpentry work when he was a teenager. "I found him to be one of the nicest, polite, kind, warm, giving [sic]," she recalled, "he was the epitome of the finest young man." Her grammar was understandably confused, given the stress of testifying at a trial when a man's life is at stake.

Speaking for the other side were two witnesses whose emotional power would be hard to overestimate: Andrew Schreiber and H.G., who were allowed to make statements to the jury.

Andrew Schreiber said, "there are constant reminders every day" since "I still live in Wichita." He is also troubled by an irrational but painfully real sense of "survivor's guilt" since he lived and so many others did not.

H.G.'s made her statement with a heartfelt eloquence. "I speak on behalf of Brad, Aaron, Heather, Ann, Andy, Jason and myself," she began.

"One of my favorite 7-year-olds lost her uncle on the 15th. This year, when her mom asked her what she wanted for Christmas, she replied that she had wings, and if they were real, that she could fly to heaven and she could see her Uncle Jason and her papa.

"I wish life were that simple. I wish that I could put on a pair of wings and that I could go see Jason - But we all know that these are wishes, and they are wishes that we have to wish because of two soulless monsters."

Her life has been forever damaged. "Every day there is a memory or a scar that reminds me of that night," she testified, "I wake up in sweats from my nightmares. I pace at night because of noises that I think are somebody breaking into my house. And every morning I carefully blow-dry my hair to cover up the spot that can no longer grow hair. I look at my knees and see the scars from the carpet burns that I got from the rape and in the back of [my] mind I wonder will it happen again."

In summing up for Jonathan, Ron Evans reminded the jury that his client had no serious criminal record prior to these offenses. He also noted that the background of both defendants was lamentable. "This was a very dysfunctional family," he states. "They fought, they drank, they drugged in front of the kids."

Closing for Reginald, Jay Greeno said, "I ask you to extend mercy to Reginald Carr that he did not extend to those four individuals."

Nola Foulston urged the jury not to be guided by sympathy for the brothers due to their backgrounds. "There is no excuse for an individual's conduct," she stated. "You can't blame your family for what went wrong in your life."

The jurors deliberated for seven hours, then recommended the death penalty.

As the defendants were being led from the courtroom, Jason Befort's brother Mark said a sarcastic "Happy Birthday" followed by a swear word to Reginald Carr, who had just turned twenty-five. Reginald swore back.

Prior to formal sentencing, Judge Clark informed the defendants of their right to "allocution," meaning they could ask for mercy or apologize. They refused it on the advice of their attorneys. Then the judge formally sentenced them to be executed.

The crimes of the Wichita Horror demonstrate the cruel depths to which human beings can sink. But something good can be seen in the survival of H.G. which underlines the awesome power of the will to live. As she told the court, "I had no choice in what Reginald and Jonathan Carr did that night, and I wasn't given the choice to save Brad, or Aaron or Heather or Jason. I had a choice to lie there and die or to get up and live. I chose to live. And I will still choose to live." In the midst of so much ugliness, her example offers hope.

Public reaction to the Wichita Horror illustrates the painful truth that so much in America is still seen through the distorting prism of race. Whether or not race played a role in the offenses may never be known with certainty but the suspicion that these were bias crimes is sure to linger. It is also possible, as the prosecutor believed, that the Carr brothers were after people who had money and the affluent are still more likely in 21st Century America to be whites than blacks

Those who suspect that the case would have gotten more publicity if the races had been reversed may have a point. It is also likely that it would have garnered more media attention if all the players had been white since this is an extraordinarily sensational story featuring a survivor whose tenacity and courage are inspiring.

However, it is not probable that it would have been better known had all the players in the tragedy been black. Both victims and suspects were black in the Wichita quadruple homicide committed Dec. 7, 2000. Like the Wichita Horror, that case is little known outside of Kansas. The public has gotten far too used to black-on-black crimes.

That white racists have used the Wichita Horror to stir racism is ironic since one of the victims, Ann Walenta, had worked for the Northeast Area Strings Academy of Wichita (NASAW), that describes itself as "a summer classical music school dedicated to the preparation and education of the African American string player."

The group has a tribute to her on their website that says "we miss her and think of her often." She was also honored by a NASAW student, Titus James, Jr., who dedicated his cello performance at a scholarship competition to her.

Others have sought in different ways to honor the victims. A memorial golf tournament was held for Brad Heyka. His father, Larry Heyka, said, "I think we had people from twenty states."

The victims' families joined with the Wichita Community Foundation to found the Forget Me Not Memorial Scholarships. A fundraising race it held September 2001 for drew more than 2,000 participants. In June 2003, the first awards were granted to Mercedes Crawford, a graduate of Augusta High School where Befort taught, and Jennifer Nguyen, a graduate of Kapaun Mount Carmel High. Crawford knew Befort and applied for the scholarship because she wanted to honor him. Nguyen identified with the victims when she read descriptions of their lives on the application. "I try my best in everything I do," she elaborated. "And from everything I read about these four people, they were the same way. It feels good that something positive is coming out of what happened."

In March 2004 the courts made a ruling on the wrongful death lawsuit launched by the families of the victims. The families claimed that the "state was negligent because paperwork error allowed Reginald Carr to get out of prison early," thus paving the way for him and his brother to go on a deadly killing spree.

After six months, the state reached a settlement, deciding to pay out a total of $1.7 million to the relatives of the victims. The Associated Press reported in an October 2004 article that three of the families were to share one and a quarter-million dollars in damages, whereas the fourth family would receive $450,000. The compensation would never lessen the excruciating emotional pain that the families endured on a daily basis but it was a gesture that signified that the state made a tragic mistake.

It would be ideal if this was a random, extraordinary case, but it is not. Carnage, cruelty and animalistic assaults take place daily across the nation. Critics have every right to ask how it is possible that the Trayvon Martin death should have reached international extremes when tales such as H.G. and her friends remain almost silent?

Where is the politician or black leader who will own up to the painful complexity of the problem and acknowledge the widespread fear of crime committed by young black males? This does not mean that raw racism has disappeared, and some judgments are not the product of invidious stereotyping. It does mean, though, that the public knows young black males commit a disproportionate amount of crime.

Crime where it intersects with race is given the silent treatment. Everything else is discussed, and if it isn't, there's a Dr. Phil or an Oprah saying that it should be. Black crime, though, is different. It is, like sex in the Victorian era, an unmentionable but unmistakable part of life. We all know about it and take appropriate precaution but keep our mouths shut.

It is no longer enough for young black men to go to a convenience store and commit a robbery for quick pocket cash. Now the store must have a white clerk that can be tortured and slain in the process.

There was no motive for the horrific torture murder of Nancy Harris, an elderly Dallas grandmother. To call it "a robbery" is an insult to the victim and her family. The perpetrator simply did for the fun of it.

If the races had been reversed, this would have been the single biggest news story in the United States. Instead it was a "hush crime." The story was quarantined to local media and websites.

Jurors on Monday were shown the horrific moment a 76-year-old Dallas grandmother and convenience store clerk was doused in lighter fluid and set on fire during an early morning hold-up.

Matthew Johnson, the black accused, watched stoically as one member of the jury covered his mouth and another rubbed his hands together as they watched Nancy Harris frantically try to extinguish the fire that would ultimately kill her.

The shocking surveillance footage came as Harris' distraught son, Scott Harris, described in testimony the heartbreak he felt as he was told while getting ready for church that his mother had suffered burns to 40 per cent of her body in the senseless attack. She died several days later.

'She could not communicate,' Scott Harris said, adding that his mother was sedated.

Johnson, 38, had confessed to the senseless slaying of the mother-of-four on a Sunday morning in May 2012,.

The footage, from a surveillance camera at the Fina Whip-In at the corner of Broadway and Colonel Drive in Garland, Texas, showed Johnson pour lighter fluid from a water bottle over Harris' head.

Before he set her alight, he stood behind her taking cigarettes and a lighter as she opened the cash register.

However, as she struggled to open it, Johnson attempts to pull a ring off her right hand but it won't budge. He licks her finger and tries again but it still won't move.

He tries once more, this time successfully. He is then seen walking away from the store as an orange glow becomes visible behind him.

The video showed Harris on fire for more than two minutes.

Black Jerome Isaac got back at a woman he thought owed him money, by cornering her in an elevator, spraying her down with a flammable liquid and setting her aflame.

This past spring, street beggar, Raymond Clark, doused a 63 year-old White man in his car with gas and set him on fire.

Melinda Sue McCormick, was beaten and set aflame in her bedroom this year by three White-hating blacks, including a woman.

Elderly couple Doris and Odis Newman, burned alive in their car trunk by a black criminal.

Bryor and Amy Gibbins' house was set on fire this past June, after a black home invader raped and bashed in Amy's head. Her five year-old son was politely reported as dying of "smoke inhalation," which is often said even if the victim actually burned alive.

Compare the Trayvon Martin case with Mona Yevette Nelson, the black woman who kidnapped 12-year-old white Jonathan Foster and tortured him to death with a blowtorch in Houston in 2012. There has never been any serious media coverage of this case.

If the races had been reversed, this would be the biggest media event in the Western world. People in Finland would be hearing about the "racially motivated torture murder" in every gruesome detail. Scores of media vans would be lined up and down the street in front of the courthouse.

Each movement of the Martin case was covered, sometimes with diagrams to show the streets and sidewalks where he was shot but Jonathan Foster was white and the Houston press printed:

"A Houston woman accused of kidnapping and killing a 12-year-old boy nearly three years ago learned her fate Tuesday morning. A judge found Mona Nelson guilty of capital murder in the 2010 death of Jonathan Foster.

"After the verdict was read, Judge Jeannine Barr sentenced Nelson to life in prison. Prosecutors had not sought the death penalty.

"Nelson was accused of kidnapping Jonathan on Christmas Eve 2010. His burned body was later found wrapped in carpet, discarded in a ditch."

"His burned body" suggests that it was burned after his death and no attempt was made to reveal the horrific death this innocent child endured at the hands of his black killer. But when a black boy dies, perhaps contributing to his own demise, there are marches and the black leaders come out and there are t-shirts printed and parents signing up with speakers bureaus.

The 1992 black riots following the court decision finding police officers innocent of wrong doing in the arrest of Rodney King 1992's Rodney King cost between 800 million and a billion dollars, along with 58 lives. It didn't matter to the collective black opinion that the arrest followed a 115 mile an hour chase and King was on parole with prior convictions of assault and robbery or that his resisting arrest was clearly visible in video tapes. All that mattered was that he was black and beaten by cops trying to subdue him.

The King case was known worldwide and brought waves of sympathy from those of all races but 20 years after the event, Rodney King was found at the bottom of a swimming pool after drinking all night and smoking marijuana. At his funeral Jesse Jackson, Jr. wasted no time in making his comparisons and placing blame on the white community.

Jackson said the shooting of Trayvon Martin shows that race relations are still far from where they should be and the persistent present-day bias is also reflected by the 8,000 blacks killed in the United States each year..

"It isn't just the police," he said. "Our concern now, of course, is too much racially-targeted violence.

But exactly who is "racially targeted?" There were 806,316 homicides in the US between 1965 and 2004, and 588,611 of them were committed by blacks, of which 179,808 were blacks who murdered Whites. Surely Jesse wasn't speaking of them. He puts a dramatic flair in speaking of the 8,000 blacks killed each year but somehow forgets to mention how many were slain by blacks.

Jackson and Sharpton give their flamboyant "bikini speeches" as I like to call them. What they reveal is interesting but what they conceal is vital. There are things they dare not mention.

Fifty-three percent of all homicides are committed by 1.2% of the population, young black males.

Black youth has caused four U.S. cities to have the record of the murder capitols of the world.

FBI statistics show that blacks murder 24 whites a week and in proportion of their participation in crime, the number is probably more like 48 whites a week. It must be remembered that the assailants in 4,000 murders a year are never captured.

Just as whites fear the potential of being victims of black violence, so do black families fear the loss of a child to the bullies and thugs that surround them.

BLACK

Me don't dip on nobody's side.
Me don't dip on the black man's side,
not the white man's side.
Me dip on God's side,
the one who create me and cause me
to come from black and white.
Bob Marley

THE BLACK WORLD

By all published accounts, living in the black world is like seeing through a one-way mirror. All the wrongs, the atrocities and injustices exist only on one side. The violence wrought against those on the other side of the social mirror are better not seen and easily ignored. The black side of the mirror represents the only truth which is commonly a litany of historic wrongs that somehow justify modern delinquency and crime.

Basil Wilson of the Institute of the Black World laments, "In the murder trial of Michael Dunn who had summarily executed Jordan Davis for playing loud music, the jurors in question took the position that the issue of bigotry or racism was not raised in their deliberations. The prosecutors also failed to raise the race question in making their case for first degree murder.

"In the George Zimmerman murder trial, the race question was left outside of the courtroom. Polling data on the criminal justice system reveal stark differences between whites and blacks, with the latter convinced that the justice system deals unjustly with African Americans while whites are convinced that the justice system deals justly with African Americans. Clearly, whites and blacks see race from different prisms."

In neither case mentioned by Wilson did the white defendant go out looking for a black victim. Numerous examples exist of whites killed by blacks who were on a hunting rampage seeking white victims and those cases were never classified as being a race crime. Where was Wilson's voice then? The killing of white victims, of course, exist on the other side of the mirror where all the guilt and blame used to justify criminality is hidden.

The one way mirror perspective of black America has little to do with logic, historic fact or defensible reason, it has only to do with self-interest and an odd form of greed.

Among the many black-themed websites continues the endless theme of reparations. Based on the idea that modern blacks should somehow be paid for the sacrifices and suffering of black people five or six generations ago. Most blacks wouldn't know where to find the grave of their great-great-great grandfather but want to profit from his toil and enslavement.

If blacks are so entitled, I presume, they would be willing to pay part of their reparation in taxes to give reparations to the Irish, Indians and Chinese who were also enslaved. Oh, but those people aren't whining about injustice from 150 years ago, are then?

So who is supposed to pay for this imaginary reparation? People whose forefathers came to America in the great immigration of the 20th century? Long after the time of slavery? Would they need to pay?

Okay, so you're black and you want reparation for the forced labors of your great-great-great grandfather. So my great-great-great-grandfather died fighting in the Civil War to free your great-great-great-grandfather. Do you owe me?

Let's not forget that some of the black great-great-great-grandfathers also owned slaves just like the white plantation owners. Do their descendants now get reparation?

To justify the concept of reparations, we need to take the question all the way back to its beginnings. Blacks enslaved were denied the status quo of their lives. They were taken from their homes and their lands and transported to a strange place. Considering that, are the descendants of those slaves better off today than if the enslavement never occurred? Which of the blacks demanding reparation would like to go back to their roots and live in Nigeria, Ghana, Somalia or any other coastal African nation? Instead of reparation, why not repatriation? After all, that was Lincoln's plan in the beginning and it was even suggested that a new African nation be called Lincolnia. Instead, it was called Liberia and its capitol is Monrovia in honor of James Monroe.

Thousands of freed slaves went to Liberia as part of that plan and one can only imagine the life enjoyed by their descendants today.

The idea of reparation, as seen through the one-way mirror, excludes the fact that everyone of all races is living on the land of the Native American. Almost every inch of it was taken illegally and by force and illegitimate treaties. So if we are to entertain the idea of reparations, we should certainly begin on the reservations across the land.

As we do that, let us not forget that all or part of sixteen states were stolen from Mexico through the conspiracies of President Polk. Few historians would disagree that the loss of the northern territories was an illegal and clandestine act. We must, therefore, consider Mexico in our consideration of reparations.

Apart from the historical questions and how the mechanics of such payment would take place, there is the question of morality. What modern black has ever known slavery? Only by the manipulation of theme and fact can it be claimed that any current hardship can be directly traced to the slavery of the 19th century.

Many black spokespersons maintain that the state of delinquency among young blacks is a national tragedy. Still, the greater tragedy is to be the normal, hard-working black family intent upon leading good lives and being productive citizens. They are also victims of the crimes of black youth since they inherit the reputation and stigma brought by decades of senseless killings and violence.

Beyond that, 36 percent of blacks, including 38.1 percent of black women, were employed in low-wage jobs (earning poverty-level wages or less). Among the white labor force, 23.4 percent were employed in low-wage jobs.

In 2011, unemployment among black workers reached 15.9%, almost double that of whites. From 2007–2011, high school–educated blacks (with no higher educational attainment) saw their unemployment rate rise from 9.6 to 18.3 percent. Black college graduates saw their unemployment rate rise from 3.5 to 8.2 percent. About 50 percent of unemployed blacks were out of work for more than six months in 2011, the largest long-term unemployment rate among racial/ethnic groups.

The economic disparity haunting the black world represents a valid cause for discontent, justified by decades of statistics and studies, not the illusionary pursuit of reparations that lack validity both historically and logically.

The average black family sends their children to school and teaches the importance of education. By example children are taught about responsibility and codes of morality. The family unit is sufficiently secure to deny any appeal of street gangs. The black father understands that there are injustices in society and in his life but dedicates his labors of today toward the dream of tomorrow. He works for the needs of today and does not share the dream of getting something for nothing as if it is an inheritance from enslaved forefathers.

The black family understands history. The long chapter of black slavery is painful to them but is seen as part of the distant past. It represents pages in history books far more than any contemporary bitterness. There is the recognition that the modern white is no more responsible for the slavery of the past than are they. When hearing black leaders made outlandish claims such as modern whites would love to have blacks enslaved today, they smile with the recognition of ignorance.

The average black family is composed of people living in the 21st century, not exploiting the past to gain an unearned buck. It is more important to construct tomorrow than to join the movements that resemble the atrocities of dark Africa more than any logical cause of justice.

Today, the average Black family has only one-eighth the net worth or assets of the average white family. That difference has increased since the 1960s, after the Civil Rights triumphs, and is not explained by the claimed factors of education, earnings rates or savings rates. It is really the legacy of racial inequality from generations past. No other measure captures the legacy, the cumulative disadvantage of race for minorities or cumulative advantage of race for whites more than net worth or wealth.

The wealth gaps between blacks and whites cannot be explained by income alone. In fact, if you compare people at the bottom of the income distribution, for example a family that makes around $15,000 a year, you'll find that the average black family earning $15,000 year in income has $0 net worth, or is in debt. Compare that with the average white family that earns $15,000 a year, and they have a good $10,000 to $15,000 in equity. That means being poor, being at the bottom of the income distribution, really means two different things depending on whether you are black or white.

The white family has a little bit of a cushion. If unemployment strikes, as it does so often to people at the bottom of the economic distribution, they've got some means to ride out the storm. They might have a car that will increase the radius of their job search. They might have this money that they can spend in case of a medical emergency, even if they don't have health insurance. But compare that to the situation for a poor black family with $0 or negative net worth. There is no cushion. There is nothing in between the paycheck and homelessness, so to speak.

If you compare, say, a white family that earns $50,000 with an African American family that earns $50,000, you'll find that the white family has about double the net worth - about $80,000 to $100,000 of net worth compared to about $40,000 to $50,000 of net worth for the African American family at that income level. So when you are talking about the difference between financing their kid's college education, starting a new business, moving if they need to move for a better job opportunity - having $100,000 versus $50,000 in net worth might make the difference between upward mobility and stagnation.

Blacks and whites really anchor the ends of the distribution in terms of wealth in America and Latinos fall somewhere in the middle.

So how do we define whiteness? Defining whiteness is really difficult because it is a default category. It's something that we don't define. And part of whiteness is the fact that whites don't have to think about race.

Ethnicity might matter but race doesn't matter to white people. And that is part of what whiteness is. It's not having to think about being in the norm or dominant group. Beyond that, it is also a sense of privilege, a sense that this society is stacked in your favor and you can do anything, because the American society, the American economy, is sort of like a banquet and you can keep going up for more helpings. That is your system. It belongs to you. So there is a sense of entitlement that comes with whiteness as well.

As an example, very few people get their job in some formal way, where they see an ad in the paper, and then go apply, get an interview and then get the job. Mostly, people get their jobs through social networks and connections. Usually it's someone you know - your uncle in the next city or a friend of a friend who knows somebody in your industry. And that is how we get the foot in the door.

Unfortunately, because most jobs in businesses are controlled or owned by whites, given the structure of ownership in America, that leads to the perpetuation of racial inequality in the labor market. Whites tend to hire whites because they get them through their personal networks, which tend to be white. Minorities who aren't as directly connected to the people who are owning and controlling jobs are left out of this. And of course, this becomes a self-fulfilling prophecy in a vicious circle.

Whites also see their contribution to the welfare of others differently than those on the other end of the scale. There is a tendency for white Americans to see the structure of their aid in the form of tax credits and not as aid, or government assistance, or welfare. But they see other forms of assistance, like reduced rents or welfare benefits, as a direct handout from Big Brother.

Owning your home, first of all, gets you a big mortgage deduction. That means you pay less income tax than you would be paying if you were renting and making similar monthly payments. Second, it probably places you in a community that has higher property values than one where you were just renting. Owner-occupied communities tend to be valued more, and that means that the property tax base is higher. That means that local services, everything from garbage services on up to the public school system, most importantly, are going to be better off in that community. So, without even having to spend your equity in your home, you are getting benefits from it.

The American government provided low-interest loans to returning veterans and other white Americans after World War II. This created a boom in home ownership and helped suburbanize America, but blacks were excluded from participating. At this same time, the government was building high-rise public housing for minorities in inner cities. The segregation in America between a largely dark inner city and a largely white suburban community is not something that just magically happened from market forces. It is part and parcel government policy.

When the government instituted rental housing in inner cities, in the form of public housing projects, for poor minorities, and then developed home ownership in low-cost, suburban communities for low-income whites, where you could put almost nothing down, they created this incredible wealth gap.

The constraints that blacks face in the housing market doesn't just affect quality of life issues and the selection of homes and styles that people can live in. It really has enormous consequences for economic stability and upward mobility and the life chances of the next generation.

Because minorities have faced limited housing options in the past, now they are usually confined to areas that have worse environment conditions, have poor school funding, have increased risk of violent crime and have worse tax bases. Plus their homes have less equity value, so even if they want to move, they are less able to afford to. Therefore the whole economic structure of the next generation can be really readily viewed in the limited housing selections of the previous generation.

The Civil Rights movement of the 1960s really marked both an opportunity and a new danger in terms of racial relations in America. On the one hand, the Civil Rights era officially ended inequality of opportunity. It officially ended de jure legal inequality, so it was no longer legal for employers, for landlords, or for any public institution or accommodations to discriminate based on race. At the same time, those civil rights triumphs did nothing to address the underlying economic and social inequalities that had already been in place because of hundreds of years of inequality.

The danger lies in the fact that many white Americans see the civil rights changes as having solved or addressed the racial problem, because it addresses the rules of the game. And many minorities recognize that because the starting line is so different for whites and blacks, it is almost irrelevant that the rules of the game were altered to be more fair. You really have this danger, where there is a complacency about issues of inequality, because we have addressed the official forms of segregation and discrimination.

At the same time, white perceptions about rights and equality often differ from blacks. There's more than one kind of equality. One is equality of opportunity, which means that as long as the rules are the same for everybody, then there is fairness. The motivation for the civil rights movement was really based on achieving equality of opportunity, and this notion of a colorblind society is based on that.

Unfortunately, the rules are often bent, if not broken, and you can't talk about having a fair shot in the game if the starting line is staggered. Even if the rules of the game are fair, some people have advantages and some people have handicaps depending on the social position of the families they are born into and what kind of wealth they have, based on past opportunities. This brings us to the second type of equality, and that is equality of condition, which is a more progressive or radical form of equality that doesn't just look at the rules but where everyone is starting from.

The notion of a colorblind society is really based on the mythology that as long as the rules are fair, we'll have equality. This doesn't recognize the fact that the rewards, the house, the Lexus, you know, the big bank account, those are not only the rewards, the pot of at the end of the game, they are also the starting position for the next generation. Until we recognize that there is really no way to talk about equality of opportunity without talking about equality of condition, then we are stuck with this paradoxical idea of a colorblind society in a society that is totally unequal by color.

There's a lot of reasons why there are enormous wealth gaps between minorities and whites in America. The most simple answer is, it takes money to make money. Part of the reason that there's this enormous gap is because whites have long had higher wages and wealth to pass on from generation to generation. And it's like a snowball - it gets bigger and bigger as it gets passed on, and the interest gets compounded. That's partly the reason why the wealth gap has actually increased since the 1960s, since the civil rights times.

But that's not the whole story. There's a long history of exclusion of minorities from wealth accumulation in America, going back to right after the Civil War.

First of all, during slavery, slaves were forbidden legally in most cases from owning anything, including their own bodies. After the Civil War, Jim Crow laws instituted policies such as the Black Codes, which required black entrepreneurs to pay, for example, a $100 licensing fee but required whites to pay nothing. Back in 1870, $100 was basically like a million dollars today. It would shut people out of business. Consequently, blacks in the 19th century through that mechanism, and through pure terror such as threats of lynching, were precluded from becoming business owners.

By the 20th century, you had the institution of red-lining as a policy in which banks rated neighborhoods for loans based on a four-tier system, red being the lowest ranking that a neighborhood could get. And African American neighborhoods were invariably given this red circle around them, and no loans from private banks would go into that system. That was a policy that was initiated by the federal government and adopted by private lenders.

Fast forward to the New Deal, when Roosevelt really cut a devil's deal with white southern senators. He didn't overtly exclude blacks from Social Security, but subtly did it by excluding agricultural workers and domestic workers, who were predominantly minorities, from receiving Social Security benefits. This was done explicitly to appease southern Senators, to exclude African Americans, who were disproportionately employed in those two sectors. It wasn't until the Truman Administration that that got corrected.

But there's a whole generation of elderly African Americans that didn't receive Social Security benefits, when in fact, it was the biggest giveaway of all, because no one had paid into the system yet.

So you had whites receiving this sort of windfall, and blacks not getting it. More poor black elderly not receiving Social Security means that working families in the African American community have to support them and pay for it. So it's not only an issue of that generation. It trickles down through issues of inheritance and having to support the aged.

Fast forward again to after World War II when you have two separate American housing policies. You have this really pro home ownership policy where the government guaranteed low-interest loans for whites in suburban America and helped them obtain wealth. And for minorities you get rental, large-scale, inner-city public housing, which of course is a wealth destruction policy.

In the 1960s there were occasional efforts to foster minority asset accumulation, but they really focused on things like financial skills, and community benefit which was, by definition, nonprofit. These efforts really didn't focus on rectifying the enormous wealth inequalities that had grown up to that point.

Until we correct the fundamental wealth inequalities, these little programs of financial education and other sorts of cultural issues aren't going to make much of a difference, because the underlying economic structure is still unequal. These are but a few of the issues facing the modern, traditional black family.

Many social observers point to outcome differences between blacks and whites, say in education, where the college graduation rate for whites is double that of blacks. Or in occupational achievement, where whites are twice as likely to have a white collar or managerial job as blacks. Or in income, where white family income is on average about double that of the African-American unit. Or family structure, where whites are much more likely than African Americans to delay childbearing past their teenage years and until marriage. In almost any realm of life you can think of, there are racial disparities.

Often when policymakers or social scientists want to compare the outcomes between black and white kids, they'll look at kids who come from families with the same income level. And when you make that comparison, you'll find that there's still a racial gap. People often point to this as something cultural or innate.

But often when we're talking about these racial disparities, we're comparing apples and oranges, because there's still an enormous wealth gap between those families with the same income level.

When you make the right comparison; when you compare a black kid from a family with the same income and wealth level as the white kid from the similar economic situation, rates of college graduation are the same; rates of employment and work hours are the same; rates of welfare usage are the same.

So when we're talking about race in terms of a cultural accounting of these differences or a genetic accounting of these differences, we're really missing the picture, because we're making the wrong comparison. We're not comparing blacks and whites on an equal footing if we don't take into consideration these wealth differences in addition to the income differences.

The black community, of course, makes the same mistake by wanting to compare numbers instead of percentages. The number of whites committing a particular crime might be higher than blacks but the percentage when compared to the population of their race paints an entirely different picture. One black blogger claims, "When the Bureau of Justice Statistics collected homicidal rates from 1980 to 2008, they found that compared to Blacks, Whites were more likely to kill children, the elderly, family members, and their significant others. They commit more sex-related crimes, gang related crimes, and are more likely to kill at their places of employment." The statement is true, of course, but who would consider it fair to compare the crime numbers of 14.2% of the population with those of 66% of the population?

So a lot of times when we're talking about race it's really indirectly race. It's that race is associated with these vast income and wealth differences. And that's what's driving these seemingly cultural or behavioral differences in the next generation. The real issue is inequality.

As individuals, we like to think that our property is a result of our talent, hard work or even luck - that it's our individual fruits of labor. But economists have shown that about 50-80% of our lifetime wealth accumulation is really attributable, in one way or another, to past generations.

Inheritance actually plays a small role in that. What's more common is something like your parents financing your college education, supporting you while you're in school or taking care of you, letting you live with them, while you're looking for a job. It's also little gifts along the way, co-signing the loan for a mortgage and the kind of things that lead to lifetime wealth accumulation. It's this enormous debt we have to our ancestors' wealth that largely explains the perpetuation, in addition to discrimination and government policies, of racial equality in wealth over generations.

Obviously, a lot of our wealth comes from our ancestors. Since whites have wealth in their family histories to a disproportionate amount, they're able to confer wealth upon their descendants, and this reproduces racial inequality.

Blacks, on the other hand, tend to have not had wealth accumulation in the past generations for a variety of reasons. But whatever those reasons, even if the current generation makes a lot of money because there's not also the past wealth to pass on, this racial inequity in wealth gets reproduced generation after generation, and maybe in fact gets worse.

The housing market is a place where culture meets economics - where values about what people want and where they want to live actually influence prices. Whites control the market by virtue of pure numbers, being the largest group. So when whites want to live somewhere, prices go up, and when whites don't want to live somewhere, prices go down.

If you compare housing in black and white neighborhoods that's otherwise exactly equal - the quality of the housing is the same, the income level of the residents is the same, education system is the same, almost everything is the same - you'll find that the white housing will be worth more precisely because it's white. Because whites are the biggest group in the marketplace, their preferences count the most in terms of supply and demand. So wherever whites want to live, housing values will be high.

The flip side is that if whites don't want to live somewhere, the value of houses in that neighborhood will be less. Think about it: if you have a group that makes up 12-14% of the population like African Americans do - or even 25% of the population if you take the entire non-white population of the United States - they can't compare with the demand created by the other 75-80% of the population, so houses in neighborhoods where whites don't want to live will be depressed by virtue of supply and demand.

The evidence shows that even if a house is in exactly the same condition - it's been kept up at the same rate, the neighborhood is almost exactly the same, but it's black racially - it's going to be worth less money than a similar situated white neighborhood.

At one time we had explicit legal racial covenants and/or redlining policies on the part of banks. Today we don't need those anymore, because once we've segregated the market, it becomes in whites' interest to perpetuate the divisions. Whites get a boost in their property values by maintaining a segregation of the marketplace, maintaining their position as the dominant group in the housing market. So once you sort of have the initial push of racial covenants or redlining or any other policy that segregated the housing market, it becomes a self-fulfilling prophecy after that.

And in fact, there's a vicious cycle here. Because when a neighborhood, a previously white neighborhood starts to integrate, even if individual whites don't have personal or psychological animosity or racial hatred, they still have an economic incentive to leave. Because they recognize that others might make the same calculation and leave first.

And therefore, if there's a rash of selling by whites, which are the biggest group in the marketplace, prices will go down, by virtue of the laws of supply and demand. So you get a vicious circle where whites calculate that other whites are going to sell when the neighborhood integrates. Therefore, they want to sell first to avoid losses, and they actually make it happen - they make white flight happen and drive down property values when the neighborhood becomes more integrated.

It's obviously disadvantageous to African Americans who want to accumulate equity in integrated or in predominantly black neighborhoods. But people don't talk about how it's advantageous to whites.

The strongest argument you can make to white people is that the current system is not in their own interest, in the long run. The fact is that homeowners and people who have a stake in the American dream are better citizens. So when you systematically shut out a group from wealth ownership, from their slice of the American pie, you're creating an unstable and dangerous situation. You're inviting civil unrest. You're inviting crime. You're inviting a situation where there's incredible tension.

When you have an inclusive society, a republic of property owners where everyone has the opportunity and reality of owning, then you create a stable society where people care about their communities and have a stake in their future. And it's in everybody's interest for everybody in America to have a stake in the future in terms of asset accumulation and economic self-sufficiency.

If we want to seriously address the issue of racial inequality in general and wealth inequality in particular, it's going to take dramatic, progressive action. Simply guaranteeing equal access to financial institutions and to housing markets isn't good enough anymore. There's just too much wealth inequality already built up, that the playing field is not level, no matter what you do to the rules of the game.

Of course the most direct way to fix the black/white wealth gap would be reparations - a simple payment of wealth from whites to blacks. That's the most direct, racially explicit way - but probably also the least likely to happen.

Another way is to take redistribute wealth not based on race but in a way that has enormous race effects. Say taxing the wealth of the rich and redistributing it through direct payments or matching savings plans to the wealth poor. It's going to take something along those lines to correct this racial inequity. Just simple equal opportunity won't do it at this point.

Wealth redistribution will never be popular. But it's already going on all the time. It went on in the 1940s and 1950s when we essentially gave away lots of equity in the form of suburban homes to white Americans. It's going on today through all sorts of mortgage interest deductions and corporate give-aways.

It's happening all around us. It's just we don't want to recognize those, because they're benefiting the majority or dominant group of Americans. If we talk about something explicitly to benefit a minority of Americans, people have a lot more problems with that.

Often whites who resist wealth redistribution make the point that, well, my ancestors didn't own slaves; no one in my family was on a plantation, so I'm not responsible for the crimes of history. But the problem with that rationale is it ignores the fact that we're all interconnected and we're all inheritors of the past.

If my family arrived here in the 1920s or the 1960s and is white, I've still benefited from the legacy of slavery. Slavery was the initial push that got the ball rolling and helped generate racial segregation, wealth inequity, inequity in job networks, inequity in housing markets, and so on. The legacy of slavery lives on, because those unequal conditions are still in place, and I benefit as a white person, even if I arrived in 1965.

No matter one's own personal views, you can't escape the larger system in which you're operating. Even if I'm not personally racist or if I can say, Oh, I've got plenty of black friends, I've got plenty of Latino friends. It doesn't matter in the end, unless the overall system has changed, because the question is, How did I get my job? I got my job most likely through social connections, through somebody I know who told me about it and put in a good word for me. And most likely that's somebody white, because whites own more companies and control more jobs.

How did I get to live where I live? I have more freedom because I'm white. I can choose to live in a predominantly white neighborhood, and I can actually choose to live in a predominantly minority neighborhood, without facing the same kind of resistance had the situation been reversed.

So, no matter what your personal views about race are and who your friends are, whites are still advantaged, in an institutional and social way, that often they don't even recognize.

People who criticize affirmative action as antithetical to a colorblind society aren't recognizing that we're not in a colorblind society. Already color matters, and affirmative action is just a way to counteract some of those overall trends. First of all, whites and blacks are coming from very different economic circumstances, due to a long history of economic and political exclusion from blacks. Also, there's the cultural and psychological legacy of generations of racial oppression.

A lot of people say that affirmative action is problematic because it's giving preference to a single group, but we're doing that already all the time in our "colorblind" society. Take the example of college admissions. Sure, there are racial preferences, but those are only meant to countervail some of the more subtle preferences that tend to benefit whites. For example, look at legacies. Kids who have a parent who went to that college have an increased chance of getting into the college. It's an explicit policy among admissions officers. Since whites, in the past, were more likely to have gone to college, especially elite colleges, that's conferring racial advantage, without ever being an explicit racial policy. Affirmative action is one way to counteract that.

Another criticism of affirmative action is that it stigmatizes the group that's receiving the aid. So if a white sees a minority kid in the hallways of Yale or Harvard, they always think, well, did he get in because of affirmative action or does he really "deserve" to be here? No one says the same thing about legacies, who get in at a much higher rate. Now, that's because race is something that we can clearly mark or identify, in a way that you can't see whether someone's parent went to Yale or Harvard on their lapel when they're walking down the hallway, as well.

So, it is true that affirmative action as it's currently designed has some stigmatizing aspects, but it can be mended. I think it shouldn't be eliminated, because the absence of it would mean that we're doing nothing at all to level the playing field, when we recognize there's enormous disparities.

So much of the discourse about race today is about how race disadvantages minorities. People hardly ever talk about the other half of the coin, which is, How does race benefit whites? A white youth is more likely to be taken home by the police and his parents left to discipline him for an infraction while the black kid would most likely be arrested.

It must be recognized, of course, that receiving a pass would be partly because of a low white crime rate that lessened the possibility of the white kid repeating the offense. The same is not true of the black offender who must share the consequences of black crime in his neighborhood.

An analytical look at problems in black families produces a list of injustices and inequities far different from those hawked by black leaders. The true problems are those that can find solutions through cooperation and good planning. The laments of black leaders are concentrated on blaming whitey for everything from the stock market crash to a hangnail. It becomes obvious therefore that either black leaders are not adequately prepared or intelligent to address the real problems, or they perceive their roles as inciting as much black resentment toward whites as possible. The result of such rhetoric is that a mounting white opinion sees blacks as over-breeding, welfare bound and dangerous.

Some of the laws and regulations of the Civll Rights period of national history give evidence to the common imagery of blacks. For example, until the late 1960's, "man-in-the-house" welfare rules denied aid to a mother who was associating with a man, especially if the man lived in her home. Although today black families have the same formal status under the law as other families, the persistence of racism often leaves black families subject to many of the same pressures they were forced to cope with in slavery. The bleak employment situation of black males has been compounded by a higher number of women than men in every age group over fifteen, and the fact that the number of black men that would have otherwise been available for marriage has been decimated by drugs, violent crime, and incarceration. The result has been a decline in the rate of marriage between black men and women.

Thus, black families are continuing to adapt through the structure of female-headed families. Through the years, in the eyes of the larger society, this adaptation has often been construed as a failure of values and morality. Thus, the black family has been described as a "tangle of pathology" and black women have been described as matriarchs, a term generally not used to describe white single mothers or white wives who earn more than their husbands.

Rather than the country considering it an ethical and moral imperative to develop public policies to address the systemic societal conditions responsible for the circumstances of black families, black families have been blamed for their own condition and have been made the scapegoat for problems plaguing the black community. Indeed, programs which have the potential to increase black economic empowerment, such as affirmative action, and programs providing educational opportunity or job training are being slashed rather than enhanced. In light of current economic and political realities, the possibility that the black family will return in large number to the traditional structure seems increasingly remote.

One of the main reasons for the current attack on single mother families is the belief that these families are responsible for dramatic increases in the costs of welfare, and in particular, the costs of the AFDC Program. There also seems to be a growing belief that when people resort to AFDC it is not a temporary status, but instead leads to generations of welfare dependency, crime, and low academic achievement. In other words, there is a view currently in vogue that families on AFDC, by their very structure, are a drain on society and are incapable of passing on good family values.

Some of these perceptions can be addressed briefly because they are based on clear factual misconceptions. Contrary to a common perception, the AFDC program represents only a tiny percentage of the federal budget. Similarly, the link of AFDC to nonmarital mothers is overstated. Divorced mothers constitute nearly half of those on welfare. Most mothers receiving welfare are not teenagers, and the average family on welfare has two children or fewer. Also ignored in the attack on mothers on welfare are the extensive governmental subsidies given to middle-class families such as tax benefits, mortgage interest deductions, and educational loan assistance programs.

The alleged loss of family values, of which the single mother family has become a symbol, is posed as an issue of ethics and to some extent, economics. However, it is clear that the current rhetoric also has strong roots in two major structures of subordination in this society -- racism and sexism.

Racism is implicated in a number of ways in the family values debate. Although the phrase "family values" is often used to decry an alleged loss of values in society generally, the phrase also has a lurking racial subtext. The term "family values," linked as it often is with welfare and single motherhood, easily becomes a code word for race just as "welfare dependency," "inner city," and "the urban underclass," have. There is an implication that black families, especially those headed by single mothers, do not share the values of the rest of society and do not pass on to their children the kinds of values that most Americans believe are important.

Racism is implicated in the family values rhetoric in other ways. One frequent phenomenon in American society is that a situation is often redefined as a problem or given more attention as a problem when it affects white people. This has been true in areas ranging from drug abuse to the problems faced by working mothers. One of the reasons for the recent intense focus on black people on welfare is that it is becoming clear that many of the consequences of poverty often associated with single mother families can no longer be internalized within the black community.

Although welfare is clearly a necessity for some people in order to ensure their very survival, it is clearly a system upon which most people, including those who are on it, would prefer not to be dependent. Welfare provides subsistence, but it does not empower people to maximize and be rewarded for their potential. When fewer persons were on welfare, there was little concern in the larger society that these clearly disempowered individuals were not fulfilling their potential, and were not participating in many of the opportunities and benefits society has to offer.

The white community, however, charges that blacks have done little to form alliances and movements to improve their own situation. It is alleged that blacks wait for whites to solve their problem while lamenting that they do not have the resources necessary to seek solutions.

As often as not, when black organizations are founded with the announced purpose of providing solutions and programs to the black community, they eventually wither into self-serving projects where a black leader gets rich and only pretends to serve his fellow black citizens. Somehow the lofty idealism that founded the organization gets left beside the way and it quickly changes into a political machine with power motives. The Rainbow Coalition still carries a "Justice for Trayvon" part of its website while urging changes in the Constitution. If the Constitution is truly important, one must believe in its content. Part of that content is a justice system that has mechanisms to determine innocence and guilt and by insisting that there should be "Justice for Trayvon," that system is neither recognized or respected.

Part of the great social problem of the black community is that it is virtually without leadership. Some critics would claim that the nation faces the same crisis but black leadership is largely characterized by a group of charlatans and pretenders intent upon separating blacks from society more than making society more equitable for all races. The dream of Martin Luther King has become the nightmare of modern black leadership. Their hate messages only serve to destroy the lives of young blacks and to make it much more difficult for the larger black community to cope.

The nation needs more black leaders like Rev. Jesse Lee Peterson who understands and shares the plight of black America but does it with a sense of social fairness.

When Oprah Winfrey made racist comments during an interview about her movie *The Butler*, Peterson was quick to object. Oprah told BBC reporters, ". . . the only way for racism to disappear would be for "older white people who were born, bred, and marinated in prejudice and racism to die" but she also said that growing criticism of President Barack Obama is occurring occurs because Obama is an "African-American."

Peterson is the founder and President of the Brotherhood Organization of A New Destiny and quickly called on Oprah to apologize.

"Oprah Winfrey is sending a destructive and racist message to black youth. She made the outrageous claim that blacks in America are still terrorized by whites because of their race. I am calling on Oprah to back up her claims and give proof of blacks being terrorized by whites, but she can't because it's not happening," Peterson said.

"To the contrary, it's black thugs who viciously attack and commit crimes against whites. Black criminals are also killing other blacks in cities like Chicago, which is Oprah's hometown. Last year, the city had 500 black on black murders. When will Oprah talk about black racism and terror?" Peterson asked.

As the murder rate among blacks against one another continues, Peterson said that successful blacks such as Winfrey and Barack Obama continue the race baiting and are doing a disservice to the black community instead of solving the problems.

"Successful blacks such as Oprah Winfrey, Barack Obama and others who race-bait are doing a disservice to the black community. This type of racial demagoguery divides the races and encourages hatred and violence toward whites. It also shuts down honest and meaningful dialogue between the races," said Peterson.

"Winfrey is a billionaire and she built a media empire with white people's support... the older generation of whites that she says need to die out in order for racism to vanish also watch her movies and purchase her products. Her success and the election of Barack Obama exemplify just how little white-on-black racism exists. For her to sully an entire segment of innocent white Americans to a foreign press outlet is racist and an insult to her own country," Peterson said.

"Her recent comments are far more shameful than Paul Deen's alleged use of a racial slur some thirty years ago. I believe that Oprah has always been a closet raci, she is just free to express her racism because she is no longer constrained by her show airing on a major network. She should immediately apologize to the American public for her remarks."

Although the issue centered around Oprah, the thrust of Peterson's objections involved the damage done to black youth and the teaching of victimization. In reality, it's hard for the white community the victimize young blacks when they're scared to death of them.

Who can forget the 1984 case of Bernard H. Goetz shooting four black youths during a New York subway robbery attempt?

In January of 1981, Goetz was attacked by three black teenagers in a New York subway station. He was robbed and suffered a knee injury but feared for his life. Two of the three attackers escaped and the third was detained at the police station for only a few hours before being released. Goetz was furious and after that applied for a gun permit.

On December 22, 1984, Goetz was seated in an empty Manhattan train. He had with him a .38 caliber revolver that was unlicensed. Four black teenagers entered and demanded that Goetz give them five dollars. Goetz refused and one of the kids snarled, "Give me your money!"

Goetz was certain he was going to be mugged again and stood up, saying, "You can all have it." He fired the revolver, wounding all four teens. He ran off the train and hid for a few days but finally turned himself in to authorities.

Goetz returned as a hero to the people of New York, all weary of thugs attacking them on public transport. Joan Rivers offered to pay his bail. T-shirts were sold throughout the city celebrating his actions.

Goetz's trial took place in 1987 where a jury acquitted him of attempted murder. He was, however, found guilty of possessing an illegal firearm and served less than a year.

One of the assailants, Darrell Cabey, was paralyzed by one of Goetz's bullets and filed a civil suit against Goetz. The idea that a robber could seek compensation for the consequences of his crime infuriated Goetz and in one public interview he said it would have been better if Cabey's mother had gotten an abortion.

The jury awarded Cabey $43 million in damages and Goetz immediately filed for bankruptcy.

How can justice be defined in this case? Was there racial persecution by Goetz getting fed up with being subjected to black violence just as were the jury members that acquitted him? Just as were the New York City citizens who supported him in his trial? Was there justice in a black kid attempting to rob someone being compensated for injuries incurred during his illegal act? The reasoning is like, "If I turn myself in, can I collect the reward?"

One of the dominant and consistent weaknesses within the black struggle to be productive and responsible as a race is the tendency to find excuses instead of solutions.

It was Jamelle Bouie's reasoning that first caught my eye, long before he became a staff writer for the Daily Beast. Whether from his own form of logic or an attempt to defend his own race, he wrote, "There's no such thing as 'black-on-black' crime. Yes, from 1976 to 2005, 94 percent of black victims were killed by black offenders, but that racial exclusivity was also true for white victims of violent crime — 86 percent were killed by white offenders. Indeed, for the large majority of crimes, you'll find that victims and offenders share a racial identity, or have some prior relationship to each other."

Is this really the point? Does the statistical factor really present a truth? According to the 2012 U.S. Census, blacks represented 14.2% of the national population and yet they committed 52% of all the murders in America, more than whites who represent 77.9% of the population, according to the FBI 2011 Report on Crime.

Blacks committed 55.6% of all robberies even though they will be only 14 of every 100 people met on the street. 40.3% of all arrests for carrying concealed weapons were blacks as well as 43.6% of all prostitution and commercialized vice arrests. Only 8.1% of the national population is black men and yet they committed one third of all the forcible rapes in the nation.

Apologists can cloud the numbers at will but the fact remains that black crime in America cannot be segregated for convenience without saying that a black life has less value and should be discounted in the name of racial image. Bouie suggests a similar percentage of white men kill white men as do blacks with blacks

19 million black men committed more murders than did an approximate 120 million men all the other races. What importance if there were more black victims than white when the occurrences are so disproportionate? Bouie's logic fails when one starts to look at actual numbers instead of percentages. Or would it be more representative to quote the FBI statistics that the homicide rate among black victims in the United States was 17.90 per 100,000. For that year, the overall national homicide rate was about four times less, 4.76 per 100,000. For whites, the national homicide rate was almost eight times less at 2.92 per 100,000.

"As noted at the beginning of this study," writes Bouie, "the devastation homicide inflicts on black teens and adults is a national crisis, yet it is all too often ignored outside of affected communities."

The fact is that it is all too often ignored and condoned by the black community itself. Black leaders like Al Sharpton and Jesse Jackson have made it protocol not to address incidents where a white victim is slain by a black offender, instead they cite the injustices against blacks in various parts of the nation. They were vocal in the international outrage surrounding the Trayvon Martin case but had nothing to say when blacks rampages resulted in massacres involving various white victims.

When challenged and asked why the death of Trayvon Martin was so appalling to him and Christopher Lane's death merely frowned upon, Jackson was true to form, telling a NBC reporter that people should look at a different case in Oklahoma last year where two white men shot five people in a black community, killing three, would be a more accurate comparison. Jackson said people "seem to have forgotten" about that case.

While there is never legitimate motive for murder, it should be noted that Jake England and Alvin Watts did go on their Tulsa shooting spree after England posted in his Facebook page that it was the second anniversary of his father's death after being shot by a black man. He wrote, "it's hard not to go off." We cannot use that as an excuse for his actions but it does qualify far more than a young black delinquent "being bored."

In spite of countless websites and posts about civil rights and past wrongs, blacks like Bouie want their crimes categorized to their advantage, citing black on black crime as if equality of races does not extend into victimization or death. True academic studies indicate something far different.

Authors writing of the Black experience such as Wilson (1987), Patterson (1998), and Ogbu (1991) – all black authors – have attempted to show that contemporary problems in the Black community such as family instability, low motivation to achieve, and high rates of juvenile delinquency and youth violence can be traced in a linear fashion to the legacy of slavery and past discrimination. The claim is repeated in multiple black-sponsored websites where such past leaders as Kahlid Abdul Mohammed are praised as being inspirations to rejuvenate black pride. His published resume stated, "Dr. Khalid trained the Ugandan Army under Idi Amin, where he was a guest at Amin's palace for two years. He also trained the Libyan Army at the behest of Momar Khadafi."

Being of service to two men who had made the list of the world's ten worst dictators seemed to be something to be admired by the black community. In their abundant praise, Kahlid Abdul Mohammed was credited with saying, "One man's terrorist, is another man's freedom-fighter!" even though the quote was stolen from Gerald Seymour's 1975 book, *Harry's Game.*

When he was shot by James Bess, another black man, Abdul Mohammad was quick to accuse the white community. "When white folks can't defeat you, they'll always find some Negro, some boot-licking, butt-kissing, bamboozled, half-baked, half-fried, sissified, punkafied, pasteurized, homogenized nigger that they can trot out in front of you!" he charged.

Like Jesse Jackson, Abdul Mohammad chose not to find fault within the black community in spite of the fact that he was shot by a man of his own race. It is difficult to imagine a more flagrant example of ignoring truth. What was really done was to fabricate a conspiracy to further alienate blacks from whites.

Linking modern delinquency to past slavery has become the staple of black leaders seeking justification more than solution.

The review of Dr. William E. Cross, Jr. presents another analysis, which criticizes the historical linkage of contemporary Black problems to the legacy of slavery as being a problematic and dubious view of Black history. His writings review the evidence that contests the legacy of slavery thesis. There is very little historical evidence, for example, that blacks as a whole resisted formal educational opportunities in the immediate aftermath of slavery. On the contrary, the educational demands that the masses of ex-slaves placed on themselves and on the larger society can only be viewed as a social movement for education.

The attitudes and behavior of the ex-slaves showed a motivation toward achievement in education for themselves and their children that was a centerpiece of their standards for personal excellence and informed involvement in the political, economic, cultural, and religious arenas of the new, free society. The ex-slaves took advantage of the material and funding support provided by the Federal Freedman's Bureau and cooperated with educational agents from northern benevolent societies. Blacks left slavery with the social capital and motivation for achievement that was needed for rapid acculturation into mainstream America.

Retired attorney and current blogger, John Hubbuch claims, "there is an undercurrent thought that maybe African Americans should somehow try harder to improve their situation. After all, the law of the land has prohibited discrimination for decades. In addition, there are many social programs that benefit black Americans.

"The answer is slavery. No other immigrant group came to this continent as slaves. Beginning in 1619 and continuing until 1863, millions of Africans were imported to these shores as commodities to be bought and sold. A vast legal, social and economic infrastructure was created to preserve and maintain the right of one man to own another."

If it was intended to be convincing, it failed on several major issues. European slavery, for example, was not exclusive to blacks. Paraguayan Indians were among the favorites of Spain and the first Indian encountered by the settlers to the New World spoke English because he had been a slave in England earlier. The Jews were enslaved for hundreds of years in Egypt, Babylonia and Rome.

Slavery was not the diabolical invention of Southern plantation owners but was a global institution existing for centuries before the black man came to the United States.

The story of Anthony Johnson serves to put slavery as it existed in perspective and was used in the Oscar winning film, "12 Years a Slave." Johnson was black, having been captured by neighboring tribesmen in Angola and sold to a freighter heading to the New World. He gained his freedom 14 years later and promptly paid for an indentured black man from Africa and later claimed he was his slave.

The indentured man, one John Casor, had left Johnson to work for a man named Robert Parker. Johnson quickly claimed that Parker had stolen his slave and the matter went to court where Johnson won and a black man was the master of a black slave. The court decision read, "This daye Anthony Johnson negro made his complaint to the court against Mr. Robert Parker and declared that hee deteyneth his servant John Casor negro under the pretence that said negro was a free man. The court seriously consideringe and maturely weighing the premisses, doe fynde that the saide Mr. Robert Parker most unjustly keepeth the said Negro from Anthony Johnson his master ... It is therefore the Judgement of the Court and ordered That the said John Casor Negro forthwith returne unto the service of the said master Anthony Johnson, And that Mr. Robert Parker make payment of all charges in the suit."

As much as it has been doubted by some black groups, the historic fact is that one of the first slave owners in America was a black man.

The issue, however, is whether or not modern crime statistics are affected by the slave experience from 150 years ago as Hubbach claims.

Let us examine the case of England that outlawed slavery a full 60 years before the United States. Moreover, slavery in England was made illegal not by revolt or protest but by concerned men and women, white and black, who essentially felt that the practice was morally wrong. Slavery was a big business and much profit was made and still the people saw fit to end the practice.

For more than a hundred years after that, the British had the policy of sending Navy ships to the African coast and board slave ships, freeing all of their prisoners. Few nations have been more considerate and compassionate to the black race than England and yet, modern England is attributing the majority of its crime to its 3% black population.

It has been claimed that black leaders are separating black youth from society. It is also true, however, that young black people are increasing the separation they have to their own community composed of responsible, productive black citizens.

Recent studies have reaffirmed a long known reality: young poorly educated black men are disproportionately disconnected from mainstream society. The numbers are significantly worse than for Latinos, Asians and whites.

"There's something very different happening with young black men, and it's something we can no longer ignore," said Ronald B. Miney, professor of social work at Columbia University and editor of *Black Males Left Behind*

Neoconservatives, of course, point to these new studies by scholars from Columbia, Harvard, Princeton and other top universities as proof that poor education and lack of job training—and of desire—are the source of the crisis. They add that the massive social spending of the past three decades originating with the Great Society has failed and feeds this disproportionate decline. The blame is on the victim, not on society.

Oddly, it is primarily black researchers who come to the conclusion that African Americans suffer a unique historical scar. The legacy of slavery and legal segregation affects their view of themselves and the view of other Americans towards Blacks, especially young Black men.

They believe that mindsets and behaviors—subjective factors—are socially driven. This is why it is doubly if not triply difficult for young black men to move out of inner cities and end generational cycles of poverty. *The New York Times, USA Today, Los Angeles Times, San Francisco Chronicle*, and other mainstream papers have interviewed inner city youth and gotten the same response, "You're not telling us anything we don't know."

The share of young black men without jobs has climbed relentlessly, with only a slight pause during the economic peak of the late 1990's. In 2000, 65 percent of black male high school dropouts in their 20's were jobless—that is, unable to find work, not seeking it or incarcerated. By 2004, the share had grown to 72 percent, compared with 34 percent of white and 19 percent of Hispanic dropouts. Even when high school graduates were included, half of Black men in their 20's were jobless in 2004, up from 46 percent in 2000.

Incarceration rates climbed in the 1990's and reached historic highs in the past few years. In 1995, 16 percent of black men in their 20's who did not attend college were in jail or prison; by 2004, 21 percent were incarcerated. By their mid-30's, 6 in 10 Black men who had dropped out of school had spent time in prison.

Who dares question me when I call this social condition an epidemic?

In the inner cities, more than half of all Black men do not finish high school."

The so-called black middle class is a growing social layer, but relative to the community as a whole it is quite modest in size. The end of legal segregation has allowed that layer to move out of inner cities and live and work in predominantly white areas once considered off limits.

This reality has focused attention on the majority of African Americans unable to leave working class areas. It is why the new studies are important and pose a challenge to society as a whole.

"With the shift from factory jobs, unskilled workers of all races have lost ground," reports The New York Times, "but none more so than blacks. By 2004, 50% of black men in their 20's who lacked a college education were jobless, as were 72% of high school dropouts", according to data compiled by Bruce Western, a sociologist at Princeton and author of, *Punishment and Inequality in America.* "These are more than double the rates for white and Hispanic men."

Robin Kelley in his book, *Yo' Mama's Disfunktional: Fighting the Cultural War in Urban America,* puts the plight of African Americans in perspective when he explains:

"Calls for color blindness and laissez-faire economic strategies also camouflage the critical role the state has played in reproducing inequality and creating an uneven playing field. Tax laws and social welfare, retirement, and housing policies have impaired the ability of African Americans to accumulate assets while facilitating white access to wealth. For most people the key to wealth accumulation is homeownership. White homeowners in the post-World War II era enjoyed a dramatic rise in property values, which served as the basis for the baby boom generation's upward mobility. The return on their investment enabled them to pass on wealth as well as educational opportunities to their children.

"In addition, the crisis of leadership in society for the working poor and its most discriminated layers. The lack of viable and effective civil rights and labor movements, both under attack, on bread and butter issues leaves the weakest segment of the population more defenseless."

The decline of relatively high-paying "blue collar" jobs in the auto, steel and airline industries in particular means there are fewer job opportunities for those who graduate from high school and trade school. The "new" jobs tend to be in the lower-paying service sector with fewer benefits. It is not a surprise that many blacks see undocumented immigrants as taking jobs they might get.

The fact that unions are in decline (representing less than eight percent of the private sector and 12% including the public sector) impacts black workers the hardest. It is harder for blacks to move from the industrial manufacturing sector to public sector jobs that pay comparable wages and benefits. The de facto housing segregation has isolated young Black men in neighborhoods that are also remote from many of the better paying jobs in the public sector

The large number of black men who have served time in prison is also an issue of voting rights. In particular, a recent Human Rights Watch report shows how African Americans are arrested at disproportionate rates for drug violations, although whites in fact commit more "drug crimes" than blacks.

Most states don't allow people with criminal records to vote. Most allow past criminal records to be used by employers to exclude people from job, housing, education and other opportunities. This has led to campaigns in a number of states to prevent access to past criminal records. In Massachusetts, for example, there is a drive to reform the CORI (criminal Offender Record Information) law. Some 2.8 million people in Massachusetts have served time and suffer from such background checks.

These few examples illustrate how institutional racism and class discrimination continue to permeate society. Young black men, not surprisingly, suffer the greatest from this reality.

> We should emphasize not negro history,
> but the negro in history.
> What we need is not a history of selected races or nations,
> but the history of the world void of national bias,
> race hate, and religious prejudice.
> Carter G. Woodson

YOUNG AND BLACK

Aaron Ellis was asked what it was like to be black in America. His answer was read across the nation.

"Before answering this, I just want to say that I love being black, I love America, and I love being black in America. Most of the time, I am just another person in this great country. But, in the recent words of one of my close friends, 'Every now and then, you get a reminder that you are black in America.'

"I got a reminder just two weeks ago, on Christmas Eve. My best friend, who was in town from Atlanta, wanted to go to a local mall just to hang out. He invited me and another good friend to meet up with him.

"So that's the setting: three clean-cut, college-educated black men in their 30s at a nice outdoor mall the day before Christmas. We were dressed fairly conservatively, wearing sweaters, jeans, and dress shoes. We were all done with our Christmas shopping, so we were just strolling around the mall to be around people, enjoy some snacks, catch up with each other, and just feel the winter air.

"After a few hours, we decided to leave. While walking out, we noticed that people were standing outside one of the businesses as though something had just happened. Mall security was busy taking witness accounts. We went in for a closer look. We overheard a witness say that a man was beaten up. Tragic, but honestly, it's the kind of crime that is common around the holidays, especially in malls.

"We headed to the parking lot. I arrived at my car first, so I said my goodbyes and they walked towards their cars. But before they could go 30 feet, several police cars sped in and surrounded us, lights shining bright on our faces. We had no idea what was happening. An officer started barking orders at us. "Turn around!" "Hands up" "Show me your hands!" They made us come over.

"They then started giving us conflicting orders. One officer would say, 'Put your hands up. We put them up. The other would say 'Put your hands down.' We put them down. But then one would say 'Who told you to put your hands down?! Get your hands up!' Back up go our hands. I felt like I was doing the Hokey Pokey dance.

"They asked us questions about where we were at a specific time. We had an alibi: We were at the Yard House and had the receipts to prove it. But that wasn't enough. The questions continued. We asked if this was about the assault that happened. The questioning officer then acted as though our knowledge that a crime had occurred was an admission of guilt. He threw accusations at us and began a very aggressive line of questioning, hoping to get us to confess to being involved or catch us in a lie.

"They repeatedly made us show them the front and backs of our hands. The idea is that if we had been in a fight, our hands would have been bloodied or bruised. Our hands were clean. But that didn't stop them from making us show our hands several more times, as though the blood and bruises would suddenly appear.

"After an unnecessarily long questioning, they finally left us. No apologies. No "Merry Christmas." Just gone. That was when one of my buddies, shaking his head, said, "Every now and then you get a reminder that you are black in America."

"I later shared this story on my Facebook and told some friends and family. The reaction to this was surprisingly insightful. Without fail, my white friends heard the story of our harassment and they were all upset and outraged. They felt that we should file a complaint with the police. My black and Hispanic friends weren't surprised at all and just shrugged it off. And this is a simple difference in the experiences of races. My white friends have never had to deal with police harassment, and most never will. My black and brown friends, unfortunately, are all too familiar with police harassment. In a few cases, they have experienced police brutality. Something like this happens to me maybe once a year. If ever a crime is committed and the witness description turns up the words "black male," every brother within 20 miles will have to answer for the crime, regardless of age or specific appearance.

"Harassment by authority extends beyond the police. In a post-9/11 world, it's pretty well-known that anyone who looks remotely Middle Eastern will get harassed by TSA when trying to board an airplane. What most people don't realize is that pre-9/11, it was black people who got that treatment. Every time I tried to get on an airplane, I was the one who got "additional screening," sometimes to the point I felt kind of violated. I had no criminal record, but this was a regular thing. I thought I was alone until I ended up on a flight with a college friend and the same thing happened to him. He told me how he had experienced the same thing since he was a teenager. He rang off an endless list of friends who went through the same thing on a regular basis. It was depressing, but I guess it was also good to know that I wasn't alone.

"I want to make it clear that I don't hate the police or any other branch of law enforcement. I find that most police officers are just decent people who have a tough job. But man, it would be nice if I didn't have to hold my breath whenever I see a police cruiser with its sirens on. Most of the time it will pass me by. But every now and then..."

Profiling, being followed in stores, people crossing the street or changing seats on the subway; it's all part of the price of sharing the image given by street wise black criminals. To many police, black is equal to guilt and no one can deny that with the extended powers given to police by Homeland Security provisions, abuses have become common.

No one knows how to close the chasm between the black and white worlds. Street corner black kids can call each other Nigger but would kill if a white person used the word.

Columbia University professor Marc Lamont Hill said it is perfectly fine for black people to use the word but not whites. He said, "You just have to accept that there are some things in the world, just, at least one thing, that you can't do that black people can! That just might be okay.

"I was listening to my young neighbor's (twenty-something) music the other night: the song "My Nigga" by YG, Young Jeezy & Rich Homie Quan (three southern rappers out of Atlanta). To me, the use of the term "my nigger" among black people can mean: "I love (or regard) you even though others think you're nothing." It's solidarity between "the damned & despised." Obviously, for whites, it's hard to be in "the damned & despised" group when you're doing all the damning & despising, thus whites using the word has been culturally verboten. Still, there are plenty of whites, often in the same socio-economic class, who grew up around blacks in an intimate way, who faced similar experiences as their black neighbors and are called 'nigger' (to their faces) by blacks. They take the moniker as a badge of acceptance, though they rarely reciprocate. It was even that way when I was growing up. That said, 'My nigger' can also have a slavery connotation, as in 'My boy.'"

One black senior citizen stated, "White folk believe that most blacks are criminals even if they've haven't ever been charged with a crime or haven't done time in jail. They just haven't been caught. To call a nigger a terrorist is redundant."

It's reminiscent of slavery and Jim Crow days whereby if a white man was walking on a sidewalk and a black person was walking towards him on the same sidewalk, the black person had to step into the ditch or road and give the white man the whole sidewalk to pass. It was a time when "blacks had no rights that any white man was bound to respect." But as Vernon Johns, the preacher who preceded Martin Luther King at Dexter Avenue Church in Montgomery, once said, "You have to have a license to hunt rabbits in the state of Alabama, but niggers are always in season."

It's easy to kill, but to be civilized is to help people live and to seek ways to end animosity and needless killing. And it's a parent and adult's duty to help young people get through the dangerous and stupid periods of their lives, where little things can become life altering or ending events. One can't fall into the trap of criminalizing youth or youthful behaviors and fads. Or using blanket stereotypes. Or fearing and wanting to kill someone because they don't look like you.

The "getting along" comment of Rodney King is no longer possible. The split in social sections, black and white, have come like the separations of an earthquake. By what manner can young blacks now be convinced that they received a false message from their leaders? How do you tell them there is no relationship between a modern white and the slave owners of the past? How can you remind them of things they have never learned?

Bill O'Reilly spent much of his broadcast time delivering impassioned "talking points memos" on the theme of young black violence. As Foxinsider.com put things, O'Reilly "tackled the race problem facing America and the lack of leadership by the president to solve these issues." Confronted with social pathologies such as high rates of violence, "the civil rights industry looks the other way or makes excuses," O'Reilly says. "When was the last time you saw a public service ad telling young black girls to avoid becoming pregnant?" He hammered away at the (genuinely juvenile and misogynist) hip-hop lyric of Lil Wayne and others. O'Reilly then harangued the head of the venerable National Urban League to "Stop the BS on black crime."

O'Reilly's comments could hardly be more distant from everyday life in minority communities. Stern messages of sobriety, personal advancement and moral uplift are pervasive at school, on talk radio, in churches and at after-school youth programs. Ironically, some of the most emphatic messages against violence, teen pregnancy and school failure are delivered by some of the most criticized black leaders.

Youth violence may be the most talked-about issue in black America today. It's a rite of passage for prominent black leaders from Martin Luther King Jr. to Barack Obama to speak at length regarding this problem. Whatever politically correct code might once have constrained the discussion is well behind us. How could things be otherwise, when violence is such an intimate reality?

Such leaders talk about crime policy differently from outsiders, not least because they are more likely to feel obligations to the people most affected by punitive criminal justice policies. Yet critics insist that if they place more emphasis on anti-poverty measures and social services, and gun control, this hardly means they care any less about the crime happening in their own communities and to their own constituents.

In almost every black organization, on the lips of every black leader and an issue boiling throughout black communities everywhere was the Trayvon Martin case. The death of the black teenager seemed to become the symbolic measuring rod for alleged wrongs everywhere. When asked whether the Martin/Zimmerman case received disproportionate attention, Jesse Jackson responded that "Trayvon is the canary in the coal mine. He is a symbol of a national pattern."

The black perspective of the Martin case takes us back to the one way mirror. There was no room for reasonable analysis of the tragedy. There was no understanding that America has a justice system that citizens are pledged to accept. There was no room for doubt of Trayvon's innocence. There was no compassionate comparisons of the horrific deaths of whites at the hands of black hoodlums. It was simply that. A black kid was returning from a convenience store and he was shot to death.

Those pointing out Trayvon's background as a suggestion of his typical behavior immediately became racists. Martin's earlier escapades of delinquency had no informative value. Being thrown out of his mother's home had no real importance or the speed with which they received a million dollar settlement from the homeowner's association.

No negative, anti-innocence postures were acceptable to the black community. Trayvon Martin would represent the dark feelings held by black youths everywhere. He would be the symbol of past pain and resentments, perhaps because his case was the easiest to defend.

One need only to turn the clock back to 1995 and review the reaction of the black community to the O.J. Simpson verdict.

"I think it's important that every now and then we have a victory," said William H. Grier, a black psychiatrist in San Diego and co-author the 1968 classic, *Black Rage*, who was delighted with the verdict.

"Johnnie Cochran is our hero," said Grier. The very different reactions to the verdict, Grier said, were, in concentrate, the black-white reaction to Cochran's controversial closing in which he called on the mostly black jury to strike a blow against racism by exonerating Simpson.

"When Cochran gave his closing, I don't know of a single black who didn't feel like standing up and cheering," said Grier. "And I don't know a single white who didn't think he sounded like some snake-oil salesman."

"You ask whites, 'What does it mean being white,' and they say, 'I never thought about it much.' Being white is like being part of the woodwork," says sociologist Joe Feagin, the co-author of *White Racism*, and *Living with Racism*. "You ask any non-white person about race and they have ready answers."

To Feagin, the glory of the Simpson case to the black community is that here, finally, was a black man with the money and celebrity to be able to expose the racism endemic to the criminal justice system, and expose it in time to save himself.

To those whites who ask what are the odds of police conspiring to frame O.J. Simpson, there are blacks who can respond what are the odds of a "genocidal racist" as Johnnie Cochran called Fuhrman, just stumbling upon this case.

"What O.J.'s money got him was the kind of trial that affluent whites get routinely in this society. With a poor black, this trial would have been over in two or three days," said Feagin.

"It's very healthy for the black community. As an African-American you can say, `Gee, the criminal justice system may be getting better, or at least you can sometimes get a fair verdict if you have enough money," said Feagin.

Black historian Roger Wilkins compared the Simpson verdict to the innocent verdict given to the police who beat Rodney King. "Both juries were responding to some of the deepest primal fears that their tribe holds for the other," said Wilkins. "Whites were fearful of untamed black violence, and blacks were afraid of the ruthless and relentless use of white power to cut down blacks, particularly those who are high achievers."

In the one way mirror of the black world, it is not important that most analysts and historians now agree as to O.J.'s guilt. A black man was found innocent by a majority black jury and that was a victory. A white man was found innocent by a primarily white jury and it is a lasting travesty.

No one made a symbol about national justice out of Nicole Brown or Ronald Goldman. The system had gone its course, the verdict was in and there was nothing more that could be done.

That seemingly cannot happen in the black world. The Martin case became the catalyst for dozens of other protests and was adopted by blacks on different continents. But if the modern American black child is angry about social conditions and the slavery issue of his past, what causes the black youth of England to be angry? Why is the black young man in France angry? Why the blacks of the Netherlands angry? They don't share the same historic experiences or grievances and yet they found something kindred in Trayvon Martin.

A young white woman was shot to death in Central Park by a black mugger. What was her name? What were the circumstances? Who was the assailant? No one knows. It was lost in the myriad cases of black crime. It was a case of a black young man demanding money from the woman and she bravely said, "No. What are you going to do, shoot me?"

A bullet tore through her chest and her money was taken from her body and it was not only forgotten, but never known as if her life meant nothing only because such assaults are too common to be news. There was no white Jesse Jackson to scream the killing into headlines. There was no Al Sharpton to make the murder a hate crime. There was nothing but silence and only the family wept.

The young black man is taught to look at life through his one-way mirror. Nothing of importance happens on the side that is not his. He is pulled onto the other side when he is arrested, taken to court and locked away for years. The other side is the reality he never knew and he views even it with bitterness. It should not have intruded on his side of the mirror of life and he will protest the rest of his life than no one knows what it's like to live on his side of the mirror.

Life in the projects of major cities leave few options to young blacks when forming the bonds of friendship. The housing units are typically homes to drug dealers, pimps, addicts and those whose tool of the trade is a pistol. It is with them that he seeks acceptance and status. In the hood it's all about manhood and it's something that has to be constantly proven. It's the cultivating field of tomorrow's new generation of criminals. Unfortunately, many have no choice but to live in the housing projects and watch their children taken away from them by the environment of their surroundings.

In 2010, Li Onesto told of her experience of living in the projects with a special sense of frustration and anger.

"There's something about elevators and stairwells in high-rise housing projects. If the walls could speak they'd tell a whole lot about what generations of poor black families have had to endure. Not just the daily reality of living in substandard housing, but the whole way you're treated by the authorities, like you're somehow a criminal.

"In Harlem some of the projects are over 20 stories high, with several thousand residents. Lack of adequate city services means basic repairs don't get made, trash cans are always overflowing, there's rat infestation. But it's not just this. Horrible and demeaning living conditions are just one part of what people here have to put up with.

"There's another kind of infestation and invasion. Something way more dangerous to people's health. There is the constant knowledge that the housing authority, child services, and other government officials can come down on you at any time. There are the Viper cameras, installed in the entrances and hallways, which mean people are under constant surveillance. It feels a lot like prison. And then there's the police who serve as a frontline in a concerted and conscious effort by the powers-that-be to repress, control and contain a whole section of society. These armed men roam about, in ones and twos or in packs, sweating people on the streets and in the playgrounds. And for them, a favorite stalking ground is the housing projects where they target especially the youth.

"Just look at the reality of the NYPD's official stop-and-frisk policy. The NYPD is on pace to stop and frisk over 700,000 people in 2011, or more than 1,900 people each and every day. The authorities argue this is about stopping crime and "keeping the streets safe." But check out the facts: More than 85 percent of those stopped and frisked are black or Latino. More than 90 percent of them were not even alleged to be doing something wrong when the police stopped them. All of this is totally and blatantly illegitimate and illegal under the stated laws of this country. And it's not just in New York City that this kind of thing goes on. Throughout the U.S., they might not call it stop-and-frisk, it might not always be a stated policy. But for millions of black and Latino people, especially the youth, getting stopped, harassed, and made to "assume the position" is a basic fact of life—where if you're "lucky" you won't end up being brutalized or killed. But if you're not, the police report chronicling the last moments of your life might say you were shot because you made a "furtive movement," "looked like a suspect," or doesn't list any reason at all.

"This is one step in a pipeline that has locked 2.3 million people in prison. This is one of the "entry points" for a whole repressive trajectory—where the cops, the courts, the whole legal system—feeds mass incarceration.

"Anyone who reads the basic statistics on stop-and-frisk should be horrified and outraged. But these facts only tell a scrap of the whole story. When I talk to Jessie, who has lived in one of the projects in Harlem, she gives me a vivid picture of what this means for people. Jessie [not her real name] has a teenage son who has been a constant victim of stop-and-frisk police harassment and brutality. When we knock on her door she is literally packing up her apartment, getting ready to move. She is being kicked out of public housing because she has been deemed an "undesirable tenant." Why? Because her son has been arrested too many times by the police.

"At first Jessie says she can't talk right now, she's too busy getting ready to move. But then, within five minutes, the stories start pouring out.

"She starts talking about how the police are always jacking up her son and other youth, just 'cause they're hanging around outside the buildings. The police come up with all kinds of pretexts—there was a robbery, they found a gun in the trash can; usually nothing that has anything to do with the kids they're harassing. Jessie says she has actually been banned from the precinct. She says:

"They banned me, said if I didn't leave they were going to arrest me—because I was saying you're dirty, you're fucking corrupt, you're trying to murder our children and they didn't like the words coming out of my mouth. They trying to take our kids from us. And now they're trying to threaten them, take them into the staircase and go in their clothes. They touch their personal parts, they pull their pants down. They bring them up in the elevator and take them into the staircase cause they can't do it any other [legal] way, and they take off their clothes to make sure they don't have anything on them. So they do it the illegal way. This has happened to my son twice. When they don't find anything they give them a loitering ticket. And then you have to go to court, you got to answer these tickets cause if you don't answer these tickets, once you get like two or three, then a warrant comes out. Then they come get you.

"If I have to go to jail, I'll go to jail. They can't tell me I can't be there for my son. I get very belligerent because I want everybody to know that they're trying to kill our children, they're trying to destroy our children. So now, 'cause they can't catch them for something they're taking them into the staircases and stripping them naked.

"My son has had a case since 2009, there's no reason a case should be in court from 2009, we're going to 2012. But they keep that case open so they can catch him for something else and then they can charge him like that, adding on when he goes to court for a serious case, which was actually a school fight."

"And she tells me about how this has really badly affected her son getting a job and staying in school.

"My whole thing about this case is the fact that he can't go get a job nowhere cause he has an open case. Close it—either you charge him or let him go. The job thing is he has a record and that's going to stand against him, as long as that case is open. [When he goes for a job] they have asked him if he has any cases open and he says yes."

"Jessie tells me she has lived in these projects since she was five years old. She's now 50 and being forced out.

"They keep harassing me and because with the harassment and the arrests, Housing [Authority], they said to me you need to put your child out of your house, because he's been arrested, he has a record. You're not allowed to be in this housing if they feel you're 'undesirable.' I'm considered 'undesirable.' One of the big things was my son was arrested when he was visiting somebody. They busted down the door and they found guns, they found weed in the house. They arrested everybody in the house. And I had to fight, fight, fight. I had to get a lawyer. Because they tried to charge my son. No, my son was not participating, he was just there. They took me to housing court—they got me for that. They made a decision, they took me to court, they voted against me... The housing court took *me* up on charges too, for him being there [in the apartment that was raided]."

"I'm deemed undesirable too. Housing court decided against me. What they did was they said your lease is terminated. But mind you, the kicker is, I took my case to the state Supreme Court and they backed housing up."

"We've been standing out in the hallway this whole time and Jessie goes back into the apartment, then quickly comes back out holding what looks to be about a three-inch-thick pile of paper. She says:

"See this. This is my case against the New York City Housing Authority. I have so many pages it just drives me crazy. This has been going on a year and a half. But my thing is, my son has never been to jail. So how would you come to that decision when he has never been to jail. He's never been convicted."

"I say, and even if he had been convicted of something, why does that give them the right to deem you "undesirable," to kick you out.

"Because I refused to put my child in the street."

"And if you had kicked him out would they have let you stay?

"No, they still wouldn't let me. At the end of the time, I took him off the lease and let him go somewhere else. But it didn't matter."

"Jessie has a lot of stories—she's just telling me a few. There was the time they came banging on her door, looking for her son. She tells this one with an ironic, comical edge.

"One time they came to my house. Boom, boom. Boom, boom. My son is in jail [at the time], mind you. 'Open the door, open the door.' I'm looking through my peephole. 'Open my door for what? I'm not opening my door, not me, you're not coming in my house.' [They say,] 'Open the fucking door.'

"I finally opened the door. They got a sergeant because he had on a white shirt and he was like, 'you need to open the door now.' So when I opened the door I yelled to my neighbor to come out cause I had to have a witness. The police said to me, 'your son just robbed somebody.' And my son was in jail! If my son would have been home, he would have been arrested and charged with robbery. They said they saw him. I said how could my son have robbed someone when he's in jail, motherfucker."

"This whole time I was talking with Jessie, her next door neighbor, Marleen [not her real name], has been popping in and out of her apartment, getting in on the conversation, adding detail to these stories. She too has a son who's a victim of police harassment. Marleen starts talking about how people are not allowed to walk up and down the stairs, that they have to take the elevator. The VIPER surveillance cameras are up all over the entrances and hallways, but not in the staircases. She says they can't even just use the staircases to go up or down a couple of stories. And when I ask her why, she shrugs her shoulders and says, "They just tell us what we can't do."

"She tells her own horror story of how her apartment was raided by the police.

"They busted the door down. And they never found nothing but they ripped up the house. They lined everyone against the wall in the hallway. People heard the commotion and came out and they told everyone to go back inside. They dragged one person out [of my apartment] with a gun pointed to his head."

"Jessie recounts, "I opened the door and saw the whole family lined up in handcuffs."

"Then Marleen says something that kind of concentrates in a way, the absolute outrageousness of the almost matter-of-fact, daily, fascistic repression they're subjected to.

"She tells me that when the kids go out to the store, mothers use binoculars to watch them because they're afraid of what might happen to them with the police.

"Just think about that for a moment. Mothers are buying binoculars. They're standing at the window, looking down, watching in anticipation, as their sons and daughters go outside to get something at the store. They need to know that their kids are all right, that they are going to come back—and not just disappear after being stopped and frisked. They know that if something bad does happen, they need to be a witness.

"One of the things that keeps coming through in all these stories is how the police not only brutalize you, but they seem to make a sport of really trying to do everything they can to *humiliate* the people, especially the youth. And the people know it and deeply *feel* this. Jessie tells of one time when the police chased down her son and were beating him. She came out to try and get them to stop and Jessie says, "That's when they made the remark, go the fuck back to the projects where you belong."

"Jessie tells the story of how the police take the youth into the staircase and make them take off their clothes. She said, "My son told me, they humiliate you when they catch you. That's the word he used. And if you run from them they might shoot you."

"They don't want a loudmouth. But now I know it's my time to move because my son said, 'Ma please be quiet. I love you.' He told me that they always talk shit to him. He's like, 'When I'm outside I got to deal with them telling me about you. [They say,] your mother is a bitch, your mother better keep her mouth shut and then they harass him some more.' So when I see them I don't want to say nothing because I don't want to cause him shit."

"Jessie has to get back to packing. But before we leave she makes clear to us that, even though she's being forced out, she isn't giving up. In fact she says, now she will have time to get more involved in things like the struggle against stop-and-frisk."

The projects are filled with tales of the gestapo-like treatment of the police. It's not just in New York but in other major cities as well. Police view the projects as the headquarters of violent gangs, the bee hive of new generations of deadly criminals.

"People don't understand," one Knoxville, Tenn. police sergeant told me, "this is a war. If you go into the projects with a nice, friendly approach, one of them will shoot you. It's happened. You need to go in there prepared and on guard. Statistically, they are the enemy. Sure, it's not all of them but many times the good ones are in the same family with the bad guys. We try to weed them out but new ones keep coming."

The New York City Housing Authority has been the subject of many studies and has its share of critics. It is a governmental entity with a complicated funding structure that since its inception has used federal, state and local funding. Early on, the housing authority covered most of its operating expenses from rents, and did its best to attract and keep paying tenants. They even put a cap, 30 percent, on the number of tenants on welfare.

Mayor Fiorello LaGuardia hoped public housing would supplant the slum landlords he saw plaguing the city. But landlords and real estate interests claimed the city was taking away their middle-income paying tenants.

"Look at the scale of the plans of the early years," said professor Nick Bloom, with the New York Institute of Technology, referring to large complexes like the Queensbridge Houses, with 3,142 apartments and the Red Hook Houses with 2,545 apartments.

"They're really not just about building transitional housing. They really had the goal, much like happened in England, of pushing out landlords from the working class rental market."

At the same time, the balance of black and white residents was steadily sliding. Every year since such records began in 1946, the number of white residents decreased at Queensbridge as the number of blacks increased.

Experts say this was in part because there was more available housing for whites, many of whom moved out of urban centers and into suburbia in the 1950s. And although the 1944 G.I. Bill bolstered home ownership with low-cost mortgages in the suburbs, blacks were routinely discriminated against living in certain neighborhoods.

"Change in the racial complexion, quite literally, of public housing residents coincided with the boom in American suburbs," said Owen Gutfreund, director of the Urban Affairs program at Hunter College.

At the same time, advocates argued that subsidized housing should go to the neediest residents, said Bloom. "Emergency cases or the homeless, moved up the (NYCHA) waiting list very quickly and moved into public housing very rapidly."

By the 1960s, NYCHA had made it harder for higher income tenants to stay and easier for the poor and homeless to enter public housing. In 1961, rent was capped at 25 percent of a tenant's income.

But nothing did more to change life in New York public housing than a 1971 lawsuit brought by a couple evicted for keeping a dog illegally. The resulting consent decree, known as Escalera, tied NYCHA's hands by making it difficult to evict tenants who broke NYCHA rules.

One housing official told Fritz Umbach, a specialist in criminal history of New York and professor at John Jay College, that with this ruling "they couldn't even evict Jack the Ripper."

In the '70s and '80s, as the drug epidemic gripped the projects, crime in NYCHA exploded, and the stereotype of the projects as dangerous was cemented in the public's imagination.

But some experts were quick to point out that welfare tenants weren't necessarily more likely to commit crimes than paying tenants — it had just become harder for the community to police itself.

The culture at NYCHA was also changing. Tenants hd to fear fines from the housing police for minor infractions like playing ball on the grounds, walking on the grass or stepping on the benches. NYCHA police could also fine tenants for hanging their laundry out to dry or poor housekeeping.

But by the 1980s crime in NYCHA spiked "ferociously," Umbach said. "And the police force and the residents begin to go their separate ways."

There are times when young blacks seem to understand their plight better than all the experts combined. Instead of assembling data and drawing conclusions, they go to the heart of the matter and tell what has impacted their lives.

Education Today interviewed a 13-year-old named Prince and asked about education and his life.

"The rap culture teaches young black males to live a life on the street and not worry about education. Without an education, I will be in the street asking for money.

"Black males aren't successful because of drugs and stuff. Their parents aren't doing right. They see their parents and friends smoking and cursing. They do the same thing. They want to be just like their friends."

Prince recognized the importance of a positive home environment and the influence it has on young lives "because their parents weren't there for them. If you don't learn something when you're young, when you grow up, it might be hard to change."

By Prince's message it is easy to realize that the rapsters don't care about the lives they affect or even destroy. They get their money and convince themselves they are not responsible for the human rubble left behind. Recording companies share that opinion of immunity and continue to churn out the negative messages that inspire young people to be the worst they can be.

Failing to plan
is planning to fail
ALAN LAKEIN

THE JOURNEY WITH NO DESTINATION

It is difficult to understand the sub-culture of black street youth. While complaining of the number of black arrests as compared to whites and the length of sentencing by courts, they then glorify ex-convicts and the destructive conduct that led him to prison.

Upon being booked into jails, guards would remove a prisoner's belt and other personal property items. The result was that some blacks had the problem of their pants sliding down their hips and exposing their underwear. Later, the same lowered pants and exposed boxers became the black fashion statement that advertised a jail experience as if it gave special status and prestige.

It is legitimate to ask why every negative example is embraced by black kids as their logo and theme? The negativism of gangsta rap. The negativism of demeaning each other with the word "Nigga'." The negativism of disgraceful conduct toward women. And by accepting the negative implications of their surroundings as the ideal, what is the final objective they hope to reach?

If you don't know where you're going, you'll never get there. The design of the normal life is to reach specific goals; to be educated, to have a job, to marry, to have children, to save for retirement, etc. Life is so ordered in able to be lived in happiness and comfort.

It is propaganda alone that says such goals are unobtainable to the black world. As a child, Oprah Winfrey wore dresses her mother sewed out of potato sacks.

Kenneth Frazier got a job as a youth selling newts and tadpoles from a local aquarium. He continued to work and study until he graduated with a law degree from Penn State. He tried to pay society back for his achievements and as a pro bono lawyer, he was responsible for the release of a wrongly accused Alabama man from death row. Today he is the CEO of the pharmaceutical giant, Merck & Co. and one of the nation's business leaders.

Ursula Burns came out of the New York City projects to be the CEO of Xerox and to be listed as the 14th most powerful woman in the world.

Sarah Breedlove was also known as Madam Walker, and although she was a black woman living in a time of the greatest discrimination against blacks, she was the first woman in America to be a millionaire without inheriting the money from others.

The CEO of American Express is Kenneth Chenault, a black man who worked his way up the ranks to reach its highest level.

These and thousands of other examples exist of those who, regardless of skin color, were determined to succeed in life and did it. So we are left with a greater question: "If there had never been slavery or discrimination, would we still have the number of black crimes that we have today?" Do we not still have the unanswered question of why nations where blacks never had the slavery experience still produce the highest level of crimes?

All the blacks in Israel are immigrants with no history of slavery and yet the June 1, 2012 issue of the Jewish Daily Forward carries the story:

"A crime wave blamed on Africans, including two recent rapes, has stoked long-standing hostility toward the country's estimated 60,000 illegal African immigrants and sparked an ugly wave of retaliatory violence against them.

"Tel Aviv police say that on May 15, several African men sexually assaulted a woman. Two days later, authorities announced the arrests of two African immigrants suspected of raping a 15-year-old girl in Tel Aviv on April 25. A third man allegedly held the girl's boyfriend as the rape took place, police said.

"The arrests sparked a major outcry among ordinary Israelis about a supposed crime wave engineered by Africans, and a racially tinged debate about the role of immigrants in Israeli society. In recent weeks, several Molotov cocktails have been tossed at African targets in Tel Aviv, including an apartment block and a kindergarten building. No one was hurt.

"After touring south Tel Aviv neighborhoods where large numbers of Africans live, Israel's police chief, Yohanan Danino, on May 16 blamed a perceived uptick on crime squarely on illegal African immigrants.

"Every time I come here, I see the numbers keep growing," he said. "They have caused the surge in crime."

"Harel Locker, director-general of the Prime Minister's Office, accompanied Danino and said that the immigrants pose a "security and strategic problem." Press reports quoted unnamed officials as claiming that 40% of Tel Aviv crimes are committed by illegal immigrants.

"On May 22 a few dozen south Tel Aviv residents held a demonstration calling for deportation of all illegals and criticizing aid organizations that help them.

"One woman who has lived in south Tel Aviv for 27 years held a banner declaring "They rape girls and elderly women, murder, steal, stab, burglarize. We're afraid to leave home."

"There is no question that Israel's African population is growing quickly. Tens of thousands of Africans have slipped over Israel's border with Egypt since 2005. Approximately two thirds come from Eritrea, where a harsh regime continues to commit severe human rights violations. A quarter come from Sudan, where tribal violence, ethnic cleansing and human rights violations are rife.

Hard-line politicians have quickly seized on the wave of public antagonism toward African immigrants. Abstract concerns about immigration and demographics have long been a concern in a country that prides itself on being both Jewish and democratic. But the more explosive issues of race and crime have raised the temperature dramatically.

"Most of the African [immigrants] are criminals," Interior Minister Eli Yishai, leader of the ultra-Orthodox Shas party, told Army Radio, using the common term "infiltrators" to refer to immigrants. "I would put all of them, without exception, into a prison or other holding facility, and from there give each of them a grant and send them back to their countries." Several other lawmakers are racing to be the first to draw up legislation to mandate deportations."

Some of the nation's political leaders have called for a program that would provide jobs for the African immigrants.

Interior Minister Eli Yishai blasted the plan as the ill-conceived work of liberal "bleeding hearts."

"Why should we provide them with jobs? I'm sick of the bleeding hearts, including politicians," Yishai said, "Jobs would settle them here, they'll make babies, and that offer will only result in hundreds of thousands more coming over here."

Israel's problems are being echoed across the globe. The Federale reported under the headline, "Black Crime Wave in Japan:"

"Four black teenagers tried to kill a woman in Japan by stretching a rope accross a road. A motorcyclist ran into the rope and crashed, suffering a serious head injury.

"While the news reports don't mention race, the fact that race was not mentioned is proof enough. The U.S. government tried to shield the thugs, but they eventually turned the teenagers over to Japanese police. Interestingly enough, the Japanese went to extraordinary lengths to prohibit photography of the thugs, even creating a tarp covered entrance to the police station. The ever politically correct U.S. military also did their best by bringing the thugs to the police in a blacked out van.

"Initially, the U.S. government tried to argue that the thugs were protected from arrest by a treaty that regulates criminal proceedings against military personnel in Japan. Though they are dependents, and one is an adult, the U.S. government thought that they enjoyed the same protections, but, of course, that is not true, as the treaty does not cover civilian employees of the U.S. government in Japan or any other person.

"Black crime is a continual problem in foreign countries with a U.S. military presence, both military personnel and dependents. It seems that that is our only export."

The British National Party reports:

"The thirteenth stabbing death of a black youth this year in London yesterday has highlighted the black crime wave crisis which is sweeping London and other major cities in Britain.

"In the latest incident, 15-year-old Zac Olumegbon was murdered near Park Campus School in West Norwood, south London in a frenzied attack by members of a rival black gang.

"Olumegbon was a pupil at the school, which was set up for what the controlled media have politely called "some of London's most troubled teenagers, who have been excluded from mainstream education."

The article adds, "the *Daily Mail* shows that of the 225 people aged under 18 proceeded against for knife crime in London between 1 April and 30 June that year, 124 were black, 18 were of mixed race, 14 were Asian, 6 were of some other group, 60 were white and 3 were not identified by race."

Again and again nations protest the rising events of black crime and again, these are nations where blacks had no history of slavery. The obvious question must remain unanswered because its implications are too volatile to consider.

At the same time, are we not conditioned by the post Civil Rights era to be especially cautious about making any potentially offensive remarks about blacks? The fear of being labeled a racist leads to a silence easily interpreted as acceptance.

Whites sharing this I'm-not-a-racist syndrome were sucked into the Trayvon Martin protests, all the while ignoring the fact that 41 people in Chicago were shot between the Friday morning and Monday morning of the Martin affair. Even former NAACP leader Rev. C. L. Bryant said that Al Sharpton and Jesse Jackson were misleading by suggesting there was an epidemic of "white men killing black young men."

"The epidemic is truly black-on-black crime," he said. "The greatest danger to the lives of young black men are young black men."

Black apologists attempt to minimize black-on-white crime by using the weary statement that more whites kill whites than blacks killing whites. Considering that there are more than four times more whites than blacks, the fact should be obvious, however misleading. When viewing the situation from percentages, however, we begin to see just how prolific blacks have been in attacks on whites.

Just as newspapers in Mexico were fearful of printing stories about cartel attacks for fear of reprisals, so has much of the black-on-white crimes gone unreported.

Two Virginian-Pilot newspaper reporters were set upon and beaten by a mob of young blacks. The story wasn't even covered by their own newspaper.

A black mob assaulted, knocked unconscious, disrobed and robbed a white tourist in downtown Baltimore. Black mobs have roamed the streets of Denver, Chicago, Philadelphia, New York, Cleveland, Washington, Los Angeles and other cities, making unprovoked attacks on whites and running off with their belongings.

Racist attacks have been against not only whites but also Asians. Such attacks include the San Francisco beating death of an 83-year-old Chinese man, the pushing of a 57-year-old woman off a train platform and playing the knock out game with a 59-year-old Chinese who died from the cowardly attack.

For years, Asian school students in New York and Philadelphia have been beaten up by their black classmates and called racist epithets.

In spite of the facts and numbers, websites continue to insist that black-on-white crime is a myth and it is blacks who are victimized by whitey. To continually bring the slavery issue into the problem as a motive or cause is much like Jews going to Germany and attacking Germans at every opportunity. American Indians should be attacking whites with the same frequency and ferocity – perhaps more.

But that doesn't happen. It's only the blacks that seem to find a need to express displeasure and resentment with fists and knives.

Historically, it would have made a much different society had blacks been allowed to immigrate to America instead of coming in chains. By simply considering the time required to make major social changes, it is apparent that more than 150 years is needed to level the playing field when it comes to race in America. Until then you will have people still being outraged at their lot in life compared to most other Americans who do not have the same struggles.

It took generations to establish slavery as an international business and it will take many generations to create a color blind society.

As blacks roam the streets, form gangs, join gangs, march in deadly mobs through cities and perform atrocities minimized as mere crimes, one must ask what is the final goal? The organization needed to create a drug-dealing gang somehow could not have been used to create a progressive program for the welfare of blacks everywhere?

The entire chronicle of black conduct across the nation, indeed across the world, appears to be that journey without a destination. To wait for the world to change in conformity to black dreams is no different than to search for the witch doctor's cures. In the end everyone is the architect of their destiny. The concept that "I commit crimes today because maybe someone in your white past owned slaves" not only defies all logic but rings of a definite mental deficiency.

The Angry White Dude writes:

"I don't like the fact that there was slavery in America any more than you do. But it wasn't me and it wasn't you. Wasn't my parents nor yours. Nor our grandparents or even great-grandparents. In fact, my family never owned slaves nor did 95+% of Americans who lived during that time. If blacks are able to blame their problems on slavery, then I should be able to blame all my problems on the English King Edward Longshanks who stole and enslaved the lands of my Irish forefathers. Yeah, that's it! The English are holding me down!

"There's two reasons we still hear about slavery every day in America. 1. There's money in it. Professional race-baiters like Jesse Jackson and Al Sharpton and numerous black preachers join a legion of professional liberal, black 'journalists' to propagate victim-status among the black community. These race-baiters are much more dangerous to blacks than white people ever could be. These evils teach those who listen that the "system is against them" and they cannot make it without massive government support. The race-baiters excuse bad black behavior that would never be tolerated by other races in society. The lessons learned by young blacks at an early age from the race-baiters is they can never be successful because of slavery and white people and they will never be held responsible for their actions. What a horrible message to teach a child! It chains them to the slave plantation of hatred and dependence.

"What race-baiters should teach black children is anyone can become successful in America by hard work, education and by making quality life decisions. Black children should be taught that dropping out of school, having illegitimate children at early ages, joining gangs, committing violent acts, etc will almost guarantee a life of poverty. These are the lessons responsible parents of all races teach their children. America offers black children more advantages than any other country in the world. Yet, they are taught by 'leaders' in their community that they are victims of slavery.

"Reason #2 for why we hear about slavery every day in America. White liberals know by perpetuating the myth of victimhood they lock up the black vote. Blacks perpetually vote 90+% for the political party that tells them they are victims and are owed reparations in the form of welfare, food stamps, housing, etc. Trillions of dollars have been spent on eradicating poverty in the black community since Lyndon Johnson's Great Society. How's that worked out for us?

"Today, blacks perform worse across the board in nearly every measurement of achievement. Crime rates, school dropouts, teen pregnancy, incarcerations, literacy, unemployment, blacks are at the bottom of every measurement. Clearly, the path taken by white liberals and race-baiters is not working for the black community. Exactly like they planned!

"Teach someone to live on welfare and they will live on welfare. Teach them to work and become productive and they will become productive. But living on welfare is easy. Sure, you'll always be dependent and never achieve anything of value in your lifetime, but then again, you're a victim. Because of slavery. It's ridiculous!

"Today, we also hear blacks complain of white privilege. There are very few who are born to billionaires like Bill Gates (a white liberal who offers scholarships to blacks but not whites). The vast majority of white Americans have had to work their entire lives to get what little they have. All the while having a goodly portion of their earnings seized by the government to "spread around" in the form of welfare to those who will not work. If there is a white privilege today, it is a white work privilege. President Obama would be wise to not seek to spread around the wealth but to spread around the work ethic!

"I grew up in a very middle class home where both of my parents worked. I am the only member of my family to graduate from college, thanks to my parents and the work ethic they installed in me from an early age. I have worked since I was 13 where I scrubbed floors on Saturdays at the local car dealership from sun-up to sun-down on Saturdays for the exorbitant rate of $2.15 per hour. During summers, I delivered soft drinks from 5:30 in the morning until 7:30 at night to save money. I even worked 40 hours per week while working my way through college while taking a full schedule of 18 hours of classes per week. Was it difficult? Was it a sacrifice? Absolutely! But I was taught to never look for a handout from others and to always work hard. And I have. Did I enjoy white privilege? If I did, it was the privilege to work hard and pay taxes for services for others too lazy to study and work!

"Black America, quite bluntly, white Americans are tired of the slavery and racism excuse! We're tired of political correctness and all the other airy excuses you use to keep your people down. You should teach young black kids in poverty to make good life decisions and they'll likely have positive consequences. Do stupid things and they'll probably get negative consequences. This is what I taught my children. Black race-baiters, you should try the same."

"It is preposterous to label a country that elected and reelected a black President as racist," he continues. "Blacks alone only make up 13% of the US population so a lot of white people voted for Obama. Just like white people fought and died to eradicate slavery. I didn't vote for Obama in 2008 nor 2012 but it was not because of his skin color. I disagreed with his politics. Just as I disagreed with the politics of Bill Clinton. George W Bush, for that matter!

"I have said it before and I believe that most white people embrace the MLK's dream of a color-blind society much more than black America. We don't see pigment at every turn, only character and actions. But we are tired of being labeled as racists if we dare criticize the massive black crime problem or flash mobs and other black-caused actions that create so many problems for society.

"Is it more difficult for blacks in America than it is for whites? Maybe. Probably. But not because white people are racist and hold down blacks. It is because the black community continues to follow the cycle of bad decisions and destructive behavior. Although I am often called a racist by black and white liberals for stating facts, I am anything but. I don't care about your skin pigment. I only care about your character and behavior. I also believe everyone can achieve in America if they only make the decisions and do the work necessary for success. Why? Because I personally know too many black people who are successful, including an Admiral in the US Navy I am privileged to call a friend. In case you don't know, they don't let just anyone drive ships in the Navy. But these successful black Americans don't speak Ebonics and walk around with their pants hanging off their asses. They are successful because of hard work and because they didn't do stupid things. They also freed themselves from the plantation of liberal lies.

"White people cannot help black America. We have seen the dire consequences of the Great Society, political correctness, race-baiting fools and professional racists in the media. These evil people only perpetuate the myth of victimhood because there is something in it for them! If they really cared about black America, they would teach decency, hard work, education, self-reliance, and other characteristics common in successful people.

"There is no shame being born into poverty. There is, or should be, great shame in doing nothing to rise above it. Black America, slavery is not your problem and hasn't been since the 1800's. Al Sharpton is your problem. He and his ilk are the modern-day slave masters. The faster modern-day slavery is eradicated is the day black America can succeed in America. And everyone in America will be the better for it!"

As candid as he expressing his opinions, the message is shared by countless whites across the land. It is hardly the message of a race wanting to oppress another.

Many blacks view the liberating Civil Rights movement of the 60s in terms of Martin Luther King, Rosa Parks and Linda Brown. You won't ever hear about Sara Lee Creech Smith who earned the scorn of her neighbors in Belle Glade, Florida by demanding better school facilities for black students. She was also the creator of the Sara Lee Doll," the first black doll and permitted black girls to have a doll that looked like them. The doll said, "black babies are beautiful."

Sears sold the doll in the early 1950s but Saks Fifth Avenue "refused to carry the doll for fear it would attract too many black customers."

When reading the list of Civil Rights heroes, you probably won't find Andrew Goodman, and Michael "Mickey" Schwerner who were white and gunned down for demanding civil rights for blacks. They were only part of the great Civil Rights Movement because you probably won't know that 25% of all the marchers were white.

Unknown on Black History Week will be Ralph McGill, the reporter for the Atlanta Constitution who wrote about equality for blacks in the heart of the anti-black south. Those protesting his views burned crosses at night on his front lawn, fired bullets into the windows of his home and left crude bombs in his mailbox. As he became a syndicated columnist reaching a national audience in the late 1950's, McGill was labeled by the Ku Klux Klan as "Southern-enemy-number-one."

He became friends with both John F. Kennedy and Lyndon Johnson, acting as a civil rights advisor and a behind-the-scenes envoy to several African nations. In 1959, McGill won a Pulitzer Prize for editorial writing. He also received honorary Doctor of Law degrees from dozens of universities and colleges, including Harvard. In 1964, he received the Presidential Medal of Freedom. Ralph McGill is mentioned by name in Martin Luther King Jr.'s "Letter From Birmingham Jail" as one of the few enlightened white persons to understand and sympathize with the civil rights movement at the time of the letter. He is but one of the forgotten whites that was a key mover toward the black Civil Rights Movement.

Never mentioned as well will be Virginia Foster Durr.

Raised in Birmingham, Alabama, Virginia Foster Durr returned with her lawyer husband to Montgomery, Alabama, in 1951, where she became acquainted with local civil rights activists. In Montgomery, a group of people in her town arranged to have integrated church meetings of black and white women. Locals as well as people from within the church posed tremendous opposition to the integration. In her autobiography, Mrs. Durr wrote how the head of the United Church Women in the South (UCWS, an integration group) came to one of the meetings. Opponents to the meeting took the license plate numbers from the cars and published them in an Alabama Ku Klux Klan magazine. Naturally, the women of the UCWS received harassing phone calls. Some had family members who publicly distanced themselves from their activities because such association was bad for business. As a result, the women became too afraid to continue their meetings. Even their husbands began getting phone calls from people who threatened to stop doing business with them if their wives went to any more integrated meetings. Several of these husbands took out notices in the papers disassociating themselves from their own wives. One man disassociated himself from his aunt, and another disassociated himself from his daughter. But, as Studs Terkel wrote, "Durr became a rebel who could step outside the magic circle, abandon privilege, and challenge this way of life. Ostracism, bruises of all sorts, and defamation would be her lot while her reward would be a truly examined life and a world she would otherwise never have known." Virginia Durr chose to remain in the public eye of the Deep South of the 1950's and not shrink from what she believed to be her obligation to support civil rights. In December, 1955, Virginia and her husband, along with E.D. Nixon bailed Rosa Parks out of jail after she was arrested for refusing to give up her seat for a white person. Virginia Foster Durr became a staunch supporter of the sit-in movement and Freedom Rights. She and her husband offered sleeping space to students coming from the North to protest civil rights abuses. Durr remained active in state and local politics until she was in her nineties. In 1985 she published her autobiography, *"Outside the Magic Circle."* She was also a sister-in-law to (though her sister's marriage) and good friends with Supreme Court Chief Justice Hugo Black.

And who could forget Joel Elias Spingarn? But they did.

Joel Elias Spingarn, born in New York City, was an influential liberal Republican and professor of comparative literature at Columbia University from 1899 to 1911. He is widely held as mainly responsible for settling a dispute between W.E.B. DuBois, whom he'd known at Harvard, and the followers of Booker T. Washington.

In doing so, he helped realize the concept of a unified black movement through the founding of the NAACP, the National Association for the Advancement of Colored People. In addition to being one of the founders of the NAACP, he became its second president, and chairman of its board from 1913 until his death.

In 1913 Spingarn established the Springarn Medal, still given annually to an African-American who has shown great achievement. During World War I, he volunteered for service in the army, succeeded in setting up a special camp to train black officers, and was a delegate to the convention that established the American Legion.

Joel encouraged the works of African American writers during the Harlem Renaissance, a period of intense black literary activity in the 1920s. He was also crucial over the years in pursuing anti-lynching legislation and introducing court cases challenging disenfranchisement, Jim Crow discrimination in public transportation and accommodations, and segregation in schools and in the armed forces.

During his life, Spingarn spoke many rallying words ("I have a dream...of a unified Negro population"). This Spingarn quote would eventually live forever in the history of the civil rights movement. The quote is believed to prefigure Martin Luther King Jr.'s famous "I Have a Dream" speech at the 1963 March on Washington.

Langston Huges wrote this about Joel Spingarn, "As an American, he wished to see his country free of racial stigmas. Within the (one) month, Joel Spingarn held conferences and addressed meetings in eight cities, spreading the gospel of the NAACP throughout the Middle West, soliciting support, recruiting members, and creating good will.

The Civil Rights Movement would never have reached its height or impact without the participation and financing of white America. What black celebrating Black History would know William Moore McCulloch, the courageous white Congressman who helped push the Democratic Civil Rights Bill through with Republican votes while demanding that the bill would not be weakened in any way as a political compromise?

The idea that black Civil Rights is the product of a black social uprising is less than half right. No one mentions white attorney, Chuck Morgan, had to shut down his legal practice and move from the city after he spoke out at the Birmingham Young Men's Business Club in the aftermath of the bombing of the 16th Street Baptist Church, which killed four young girls. He told them the entire community should take responsibility for the climate of hate that had led to the bombing.

The Civil Rights Movement could never have succeeded without a strong core of lawyers pushing its measures through courts toward the halls of Congress. Many of them worked at no cost but no one would know the names of Oscar W. Adams Jr.; Norman Amaker; James K. Baker; Abe Berkowitz; Orzell Billingsley; Harvey Burg; U.W. Clemon; Jerome "Buddy" Cooper; J. Mason Davis; Edward Friend Jr.; Peter A. Hall; Charles Hamilton Houston: Frank M. Johnson; Paul Johnston; Tom King Sr.; Thurgood Marshall; Nina Miglionico; Constance Baker Motley; Demetrius Newton; Vernon Patrick; J. Richmond Pearson; Arthur D. Shores; C. Erskine Smith; Robert Vance; David Vann; and W.L. Williams Jr.

White America is intent upon thwarting the progress of blacks? Only through the hate messages of race monger so-called leaders is this myth perpetuated.

In reality, race in America is a constantly shifting combination a much larger reality that is all around us, and the personal experiences of those who live within that reality. All the good intentions of white people do not change 200 years of slavery, 150 years of back-lash to Reconstruction and Jim Crow, 350 cumulative years of cultural attitudes, institutionalized discrimination, and the very daily reality of bigotry and under-representation of people of color in America's cultural and political lives.

There's something myopic, if not narcissistic, about this tendency to reduce these huge, complicated issues to the things we've personally experienced and the thing we've personally seen, or the tendency to posit ourselves as objective arbiters of the way the world works.

And yet, that is the essence of the young black view of modern life. Everything – the only thing – that can be equated is the collection of personal experiences. Life in the projects, unemployment, the quick buck selling drugs on the corner; all can be factored. Going from the classroom to the cell because education doesn't do a person any good in the reality of the streets is a common belief. Absorbing the messages of the corruptive gangsta' music because rapsters "understand" and "speak the young black language" is a typical response. The crude philosophy that screams to define manhood; I can fuck with anyone but no one can fuck with me. And, of course, there's no need to plan ahead because there's probably nothing there anyway.

The road toward self destruction is well traveled in urban America and now expresses itself in "flash mobs," hundreds of blacks rampaging and robbing in waves of fear and terror. Attacks blatantly targeting whites occur but are never called race crimes and all the while, America's black leaders have better things to do, like stir up more hatred.

One would have thought that the memorial to celebrate the 50th anniversary of Martin Luther King's "I have a dream" speech would have been a solemn and respectful affair. Instead, part of the leaders of the nation's black community used the event to stir up even more hatred.

Instead of simply using the opportunity to honor the work of his father in a dignified way, King's son, Martin Luther King III, cheapened it by attempting to stir up racial hatred. He said the Trayvon Martin killing last year, ruled by a jury to be a justifiable homicide in which race played no role, shows that America is a deeply racist country.

"The task is not done, the journey is not complete," he said. "The vision preached by my father a half-century ago was that his four little children would no longer live in a nation where they would be judged by the color of their skin but by the content of their character."

"However, sadly, the tears of Trayvon Martin's mother and father remind us that, far too frequently, the color of one's skin remains a license to profile, to arrest and to even murder with no regard for the content of one's character," King said, throwing in a pitch to repeal "stand your ground" self-defense laws, which had no bearing on the Martin case.

King was not alone among black leaders in trying to leverage the Martin killing for political purposes and self-advancement. Pseudo-intellectuals like Georgetown's Michael Eric Dyson said after George Zimmerman was acquitted in the killing of Trayvon Martin that it would be a good thing for more white children to be murdered so Americans could better understand racism

These people have become rich and famous by vilifying white people and the American system, claiming blacks are persecuted and discriminated against, and asserting that there is an invisible conspiracy of white supremacists preventing black people from becoming successful. Not everything they do or say is actually racist in any meaningful sense, but they routinely say things that conservatives would be pilloried for had they said them about people of a different race.

The weekend celebration would have been worthwhile as a historical commemoration, but activists like King and Al Sharpton decided to ruin the event by turning it into a call to action. The leaders on the weekend were largely race industry profiteers and poverty pimps, not sincere celebrants marking a solemn occasion. They rallied against evils that no longer exist.

And they ignored the evils that do exist.

As Colin Flaherty, author of *White Girl Bleed A lot,* has documented, black-on-white violence has become increasingly commonplace in recent years, despite the best efforts of the media, politicians, and left-wing activists to ignore it or deny its existence. America's major urban centers, cities like Chicago and Philadelphia, have been plagued by black race riots in recent years. Few people know about these often deadly melees because they rarely get reported.

Few had read about the 88-year-old World War II veteran Delbert Belton who was beaten to death by blacks in Spokane. Before that, blacks allegedly killed nurse David Santucci in Memphis. Who could forget the blacks shooting the baby in the stroller as the mother watched horrified before being shot herself?

Before that, blacks in Minnesota beat Ray Widstrand so brutally that he suffered permanent brain damage, and in Missouri a black mob hit a hot dog vendor in the head with a hammer. A black mob assaulted a police officer with a baseball bat, leaving him with a fractured skull.

No doubt some politicians and journalists deny the existence of all this racially motivated violence in a misguided effort to protect blacks who in the past suffered from racial discrimination and the ravages of slavery. They see reports of black violence as reinforcing negative stereotypes and setting back race relations.

But members of today's civil rights establishment don't have that excuse available to them. They aren't interested in solving or even acknowledging the problems of the black community because they profit so handsomely from them. They see turmoil in black neighborhoods as opportunities to promote change.

Speakers at the weekend rally seemed blissfully ignorant of the fact that America has come a long way since 1963 when Democratic President John F. Kennedy and congressional Democrats worked together to block civil rights legislation.

It is as if the civil rights revolution never happened and Jim Crow is still making the lives of black Americans miserable. The unspoken premise of all these self-serving rants is that America somehow owes blacks for past injustices even though most Americans today weren't even alive in 1963.

Martin Luther King III isn't even the worst offender among the race hustlers, most of whom skipped the event at the Lincoln Memorial. But what the event did was to bring together some of the nation's examples of black leadership and permit us to explore them as they really are.

A TV show host at MSNBC despite his inability to speak proper English or at times, to formulate coherent thoughts, Al Sharpton has largely managed to escape his past. Founder of the National Action Network, he helped to incite anti-Jewish riots in Crown Heights, New York in 1991. He uses the word "cracker" to refer to various white people, has ties to the criminal underworld, and participated in the infamous racially charged Tawana Brawley hoax and incited black anti-Semites against a Jewish business establishment in Harlem in 1995. He appeared on the late Morton Downey's television program and publicly used an anti-gay slur, calling an audience member "a punk faggot!" He even tried to win the Democratic Party presidential nod in 2004.

His widespread acceptance as a legitimate spokesman for the black community by the rest of the media and the Obama administration has allowed Sharpton to supplant Jesse Jackson Sr. as America's foremost retail race hustler. He was publicly embraced by Obama cabinet members, including Attorney General Eric Holder and HUD Secretary Shaun Donovan, at his group's convention in Washington, D.C. last year.

Some liberal journalists are tiring of him, though. Last week Margaret Carlson lamented the declining quality of leadership in today's so-called civil rights movement. "We've gone from Martin Luther King to the Reverend Al Sharpton, and as a leader, as he is trying to be this weekend, it's very dispiriting."

Barack Obama has long regarded America as a deeply flawed, profoundly racist country. He has attacked the Constitution as an outmoded, obsolete document written by white men. He has called opponents of affirmative action racists. In 1995, Obama made reference to a hypothetical "white executive living out in the suburbs, who doesn't want to pay taxes to inner city children for them to go to school."

He even famously threw his own white grandmother under the bus, suggesting she harbored racial animosity. "She is a typical white person who, uh, if she sees somebody on the street that she doesn't know there's a reaction that's been bred into our experiences that don't go away and that sometimes come out in the wrong way and that's just the nature of race in our society."

While at Harvard Law School Obama defended racist law professor Derrick Bell, the creator of critical race theory. Bell was notoriously anti-white and believed America has a hopelessly racist country. Obama described Bell as someone who spoke "the truth." Obama later taught courses about America's "Institutional Racism" at the University of Chicago Law School.

When a friend of his, a black Harvard professor, was arrested in Cambridge, Mass., without examining the facts Obama said the police "acted stupidly." After Trayvon Martin was killed last year, Obama injected race into the matter by saying if he had a soon he'd look like Martin.

First Lady Michelle Obama has had greater difficulty concealing her hatred of America than her husband has had. She regards America as a racist, sexist, homophobic nation, declaring in 2008, after the American public began warming to her husband's presidential campaign, "For the first time in my adult lifetime, I am really proud of my country..."

A beneficiary of affirmative action, Mrs. Obama was a member of the board of a radical, racist group called Third World Center while studying at Princeton. She was also admitted to Harvard Law School, given preference because of her skin color. In law school she embraced critical race theory, an intellectual movement whose adherent federal Judge Richard Posner has described as the "lunatic core" of "radical legal egalitarianism."

As attorney general, Eric Holder refused to prosecute the New Black Panther Party members who openly brandished weapons at a Philadelphia polling station in 2008 in order to intimidate white voters. He also refuses to enforce electoral integrity laws and fights voter ID laws because he alleges they discriminate against minorities. He supports affirmative action programs, which by definition, of course, are racist because they discriminate against white Americans.

Holder has called America "essentially a nation of cowards," because most Americans don't share his radical left-wing multiculturalists views on race. "We, average Americans, simply do not talk enough with each other about race. It is an issue we have never been at ease with and, given our nation's history, this is in some ways understandable.... This nation has still not come to grips with its racial past ..."

Holder calls conservatives "defenders of the status quo, afraid of the future, and content to allow to continue to exist all but the most blatant inequalities." They "put the environment at risk for the sake of unproven economic theories, to play to the fears of our citizens, and not to their hopes, and to return the nation to a time that in fact never existed." The hallmarks of the "conservative agenda" include "social division, mindless tax cutting, and a defense posture that does not really make us safer."

A longtime Obama idolator, Oprah Winfrey was instrumental in the president's rise. She invited Obama on her TV show to promote one of his books and promoted him relentlessly.

Despite all evidence to the contrary, Winfrey insists on blaming the killing of Trayvon Martin on racial animosity. "To me, it's ridiculous to look at that case and not to think that race was involved," she said.

She also likened the killing of Martin to the brutal 1955 murder of 14-year-old black Emmett Till. "In my mind, same thing," she said. Till was kidnapped by two white men in Mississippi who beat him, gouged out one of his eyes, shot him in the head, and dumped his body into a river. His death helped to galvanize the early civil rights movement.

James Cone is the father of it all. We can only wonder how many people have been killed by followers of black liberation theology, which Cone invented. Cone was a Professor of Systematic Theology at the Union Theological Seminary in New York City. He regards America as an irredeemably racist nation.

"What we need is the divine love as expressed in Black Power, which is the power of Black people to destroy their oppressors here and now by any means at their disposal.

Unless God is participating in this holy activity, we must reject his love," Cone wrote.

A more sophisticated version of Louis Farrakhan, Cone blames whites for, well, everything bad. "This country was founded for whites and everything that has happened in it has emerged from the white perspective. What we need is the destruction of whiteness, which is the source of human misery in the world."

Jeremiah Wright and other radical church leaders believe in black liberation theology, an Afrocentrist mix of Christianity, Marxism, and anti-white racial bigotry. Cone claims that "black values" –whatever those may be– are superior to American values.

As already described, at the Saturday rally King described the killing of Trayvon Martin as racially motivated, even though that claim was ultimately rejected by police and the jury. Apparently following the advice of *Rules for Radicals* author Saul Alinsky, who taught that action itself is more important than having real issues to campaign on, King urged action. "This is not the time for nostalgic commemoration," King added. "Nor is this the time for self-congratulation. The task is not done. The journey is not complete. We can and we must do more."

Of course, King has been dining out on his father's hard work for decades. He has frequently been criticized by his own allies for laziness. In 2001 the Southern Christian Leadership Conference suspended King as president out of concern he was neglecting his duties at the group founded by his father. He was a Fulton County, Ga., commissioner until his deadbeat ways became public knowledge, leading to his electoral defeat in 1993. He owed the federal government more than $200,000 in back taxes and fines.

Cornel West, who describes himself as a "non-Marxist socialist," was an adviser on President Obama's 2008 campaign team. He wrote in his book *Democracy Matters: Winning the Fight Against Imperialism*, that the U.S. is under the control of racist, patriarchal, authoritarian fundamentalists. He supports black liberation theology, the same set of radical, anti-American beliefs preached by Obama's longtime Jew-hating pastor, Rev. Jeremiah Wright.

There are few groups in American society that Louis Farrakhan, who ought to be under constant FBI surveillance, does not hate. The legendary anti-Semite, who says the U.S. government has long been conspiring against blacks, developed a strong dislike for Malcolm X in the 1960s because he believed X was too moderate. Farrakhan refers to Caucasians as "white devils" and Jews as "bloodsuckers."

In 1984 after a black *Washington Post* reporter named Milton Coleman publicly revealed that then-presidential candidate Jesse Jackson Sr. had referred to Jews as "Hymies" and to New York City as "Hymietown," Farrakhan told Coleman: "One day soon we will punish you with death." He regarded Coleman as a race traitor.

The problem isn't so much that leftists explicitly embrace Farrakhan. Few do, perhaps because they view him as an embarrassing cartoon. It's not often that you'll see mainstream broadcasters give him air time. The problem is that leftists refuse to denounce Farrakhan and his poisonous ideas.

When Barack Obama ran for president in 2008, Walker endorsed him. "He is the change America has been trying desperately and for centuries to hide, ignore, kill. The change America must have if we are to convince the rest of the world that we care about people other than our (white) selves."

Walker is a supporter of convicted, unrepentant cop killer Mumia abu Jamal and compares Israel to Nazi Germany. Describing Israel's treatment of Palestinians, she uses words and phrases such as "genocide," "ethnic cleansing," "crimes against humanity," and "cruelty and diabolical torture."

In 2002, Walker appeared in a documentary film about Fidel Castro. She was quoted saying "What's not to like about the man? If Fidel could dance, he'd be perfect!"

Following the 9/11 attacks, Walker urged that "love" be used against the terrorist perpetrators. "In a war on Afghanistan, Osama bin Laden will either be left alive, while thousands of impoverished, frightened people are bombed into oblivion around him, or he will be killed in a bombing attack for which he seems quite prepared. But what would happen to his cool armor if he could be reminded of all the good, nonviolent things he has done? Further, what would happen to him if he could be brought to understand the preciousness of the lives he has destroyed? I firmly believe the only punishment that works is love."

I never dreamed that at any point in my life would I agree with Bill O'Reilly about anything. In fact, I promised myself that I wouldn't. But his comments about the black issue and black leadership did fall into step with my opinions.

"The sad truth is that from the President on down, our leadership has no clue, no clue at all about how to solve problems within the black community," O'Reilly explained. "And many are frightened to even broach the issue. That's because race hustlers and the grievance industry have intimidated the so- called 'conversation,' turning any valid criticism of African-American culture into charges of racial bias."

"So many in power simply walk away leaving millions of law abiding African-Americans to pretty much fend for themselves in violent neighborhoods. You want racism? That's racism,"

I don't know how it happened but O'Reilly finally had something right. The real issue is that leftist leaders from Obama to Sharpton, to Jackson, derive their power from the disproven narrative that portrays blacks as victims of white oppression. Poverty, unemployment, drugs, violence, exploitation, all these are a product of the sins of the white man.

Yet, there is no white man alive who once held a black in bonded slavery. Indeed, we are several generations removed from the scourge of slavery. Throughout the intervening generations, we have followed policies designed to give blacks compensation for their disadvantaged start in America, including affirmative action policies and a degree of preferential treatment within society.

The treatment has been so special, so delicate, that we have decreed certain words off limits, and forbid discussion of topics which we fear would offend black sensibilities. We dedicate a month to "black history" make special mention of blacks in schools and universities with entire courses of study devoted to black culture. We have black media, black awards and black television channels.

So while we talk about stoplights and peanut butter in school, contributions of black inventors, we ignore the real issues confronting blacks in America.

If you want to help blacks, then let us address the real issues confronting children of the many black races forcibly brought to America nearly two centuries ago.

Let's talk about the black family, and the fact that as O'Reilly explained nearly three quarters of black mothers are unwed. An entire segment of our population is producing children with different fathers and without the stability a marriage provides. This isn't a problem unique to blacks. Whites do this too, as do people of all races. However, the numbers are most alarming within the black community.

Where are all the black dads - babies daddy? What are they doing and what lessons are their children learning?

Many of them are in prison. Is it because the system is corrupted and targets blacks?

No, it's because blacks, many raised without respect and having squandered their best opportunity for an education, turn to drugs and violence, welfare and the public dole, to make their way in the world. Meanwhile, black culture including music and media, enables this choice by glamorizing it, and incorporates this notion into its all-pervasive narrative. It's somehow become normal, almost expected for black to be incarcerated. Really? Since when? Since blacks have allowed this perception to perpetuate, after all, it's easier to deflect responsibility to a "system" that is somehow broken than to take each case individually.

The rest of the nation hears this narrative, and it alarms us. Blacks are poor, oppressed and angry. Blacks are inclined to criminal activity, violence, value money over family, divorce, never build families, kill one another and end up in prison.

Is this racist? You bet it is. It's a terrible thing to say, but it is the narrative that blacks swim in. It's a narrative used by Obama, Shaprton and Jackson to fund their careers. And it's a lie.

Who has control over this narrative? Why is it such a painful thing to regard? It isn't whites, or asians, or Hispanics who control the narrative.

This narrative can be changed, and it begins today, with you. You want to end racism? Okay, end it. Start by getting rid of the race-baiters who capitalize on your pain.

Next, black mothers must insist upon abstinence, marriage and monogamy. They must turn away from abortion which is the first violence that many black youth are exposed to, and certainly do not survive.

Black fathers must commit themselves to their families. They must realize that rap stars, basketball players and other celebrities get rich, but what have these people done for their households except sell a false narrative of black life in America to their blacks and whites alike?

Instead of idolizing rap stars with diamonds where their teeth should be, they should idolize black men who have made a positive difference in society.

As the current generation changes the way it relates to the world, they force the world to change the way it relates to them. The world will have no choice. It will be immediate and automatic. Black children, brought up by committed parents will learn the same respect as any other child in any other similar household. That child will attend school, complete their education, and be instilled with values that will break the cycle of poverty that plagues the black races in America.

Soon, race will fade as an issue. We won't talk about "black-on-black" violence or "black culture" because these will become anachronisms. Instead, we will all simply be Americans who share common values and morals and enjoy the same access as all others.

How many people have the courage to call this out? Certainly not Obama, Sharpton, or Jackson. They're too busy selling a racist lie.

America's black community must create new leaders. And the leaders cannot be accepted because they scream the loudest about injustice or inspire with calls to arms. They must be leaders with the sincere concern for their people at heart. They must educated and connected. They must be vocal and speak correctly. They must be the example that young people would want to follow.

They should be leaders that do not come to you from pulpits or Capitol Hill. They should come from within, from the roots of the people and their situations. They should know and understand the lives that pass around them. They should know about poverty from experience and injustice by their own pain.

And if anyone cares to listen, a black leader doesn't even need to be black.

Of the ten richest black people in the U.S., three are athletes and four are rapsters or associated with the production of rap. Oprah Winfrey and Bill Cosby are in the entertainment business. Only R. Donahue Peebles, a real estate investor, made his fortune by using his skills the way that black people need to do and he's the last one on the list.

That's a sad commentary to how some black people see themselves. Society already characterizes blacks as being in the entertainment business, basketball players or criminals and from a black economy begging for relief, millions go into the pockets of those producing the music that corrupts black youth.

It is equally wrong to believe that the black community will ever be represented by the thugs endangering the nation's streets. An episode of "What Would You Do?" gave inspiring evidence of how many black people in Harlem defended a white woman being criticized by a black. They were actors, of course, but the messages coming from blacks should be the anthem of the forward movement of their people.

"We need to move forward," said one black woman, "and we can't do it without them." The sense of social unity in a noble cause carried a greater impact than any act of violence creating fear instead of a desire to cooperate and assist.

America lives in a time of great confusion. The government that historically served its people now seems more intent upon controlling them. It was a nation that had a government and today it is a government that has a nation. The loss of some of the most basic guarantees like habeas corpus brings a somber fear across the land. Extended powers given to agencies and local police are often the cause for the abuses cited by many. It is an ironic contrast wherein whites want to return to the land they knew and blacks want to climb up from the land known to their forefathers.

The vast majority of blacks deplore that actions of renegade black youth contaminating the reputation of the race as a whole. Parents suffer as the streets claim their children and the perpetuated conditions of urban life leave no avenue of escape.

Among the most reviled black leaders is the Rev. James David Manning and his occasional comment that hints of a bizarre perception of his race. But Manning stands alone in his criticism of his own people and alone in his message of how they must rise together. No one needs to agree with his hatred of Barack Obama but it would be best not to ignore his interpretations of black history.

Manning speaks of the tendency for black men to make bad decisions. He condemns black men abandoning their families and confesses that he once did the same. He condemns the reckless production of babies without the means to care for them. He promotes education and criticizes white people for not trying to understand the black mystique. He calls Sharpton, Jackson, Farrakhan, the NAACP and Urban League "pimps" and attacks their dedication to self interest.

Manning was the only black leader criticizing Sybrina Fulton, accusing her of using the death of her son for personal profit and avoiding the fact that she threw him out of her home. He also took Obama to task for his comment about if he had a son . . . ." The bottom line is that Sybrina Fulton has had her fifteen minutes of fame but the problems of black America continue. Her rhetoric did nothing but stir greater hatred across the land, just as Sharpton, Jackson and King so expertly do.

Whether anyone agrees totally with Manning or not, what he does represent is the type of brutal honesty needed in the black and white communities if they are to ever meld into one.

Beneath the violence and anger rests the foundation of American society. It is constructed of intelligent, well meaning citizens who understand that social division leads only to the detriment of all. They are genuinely interested in seeing all people progress and enjoy the bounty America has to offer. Together they can reform and reshape the government that has abandoned them with its neglect of effective domestic programs.

It is with the same sense of unity that violence in America's streets must be addressed and ended. The guilty must pay the penalties prescribed without assigning the blame to any social injustice or historic influence.

Peace, prosperity and progress must become the themes of creating a new future. Professional politicians must be torn from their thrones in Washington and skilled, dedicated Americans taking their place. The administrative philosophy of keeping the nation in a state of constant fear must be ended and the rights of citizens restored. The leaders of the future must embrace diplomacy over destruction and peace over power.

America is still in the process of nation building and to this date it has not done a very good job. The natural wealth of the land has succumbed to environmental crimes. The hope of the world has become its greatest bully. Its former slaves were given freedom but never respect or equality. It's promise has fallen into the pockets of the power structure of Capitol Hill and corporate leaders. Its middle class is shrinking into the statistics of poverty.

It is time for another reconstruction period of the United States. It must be the rebuilding of all the founding fathers intended. It must repeal the restrictive and oppressive measures enacted during the George W. Bush administration and empower companies to once again bring production back to American soil.

The people must regain control of their streets. Youth gangs, drug dealers and delinquents must learn that no one owes them anything and that the pain they bring to society will not be tolerated. If drugs must be legalized to end the intrusion of cartels and violent distributors, then legalize it and permit addicts to buy from government stores at lower prices where drug-producing crops can be subsidized and taxes collected from the sales. If they waste their lives in the stupor of addiction, they would have anyway only with a long record of thefts and convictions that would be expenses to society at large.

It will not be easy or considerate of social grace or feelings. Moving forward doesn't mean the road will be smooth, it means it will be made smooth in time. It might mean the youth recognizing the power of their voting numbers and the formation of a new political power dedicated to all that is best for America. Radical ideas might be entertained like the British system of a vote of confidence or popular referendums.

The only current certainty is that the apathy of the new American is not working. It turns citizens into victims and thwarts every attempt at social progress, including the end of discrimination and racial strife. It permit less than a thousand people in Washington to make the decisions that secures their futures while endangering yours.

When the people come to the realization that there is no black or white America, only people struggling for survival, then hope will be restored. When the learn to help each other so that they survive together, then the future will be secured.

BLACK

ABOUT THE AUTHOR

David Ellsworth is the prolific author
of sixteen books and divides his time
between Italy and Mexico

www.ingramcontent.com/pod-product-compliance
Lightning Source LLC
Chambersburg PA
CBHW060501290526
45791CB00001B/221